Charlie Carrillo:
Tradition & Soul/Tradición y Alma

D0859207

Barbe Awalt & Paul Rhetts

LPD Press, a division of LPD Enterprises • Albuquerque

"Acts of creation are ordinarily reserved for gods and poets, but humbler folks may circumvent this restriction if they know how. To plant an oak for example, one need be neither a god or poet: one needs only a shovel."

Anonymous

ABOVE: Cristo Crucificado, 1992. Size: 18" tall. See page 105 for further details. Photo by Lindsay Holt II.

Copyright © 1995 by LPD Enterprises. All Rights Reserved. Printed in the United States of America. No part of this book may be reproduced or transmitted in any form without written permission from the author/publisher.

Color separations by: Checkmate Graphics Pre-Press, Inc., Columbia, Maryland
Printing by: Dataco, WBC Inc. Company, Albuquerque, New Mexico
Typesetting & Design by: Paul Rhetts and Barbe Awalt

Authors' note: Unless otherwise noted all retablos in this book are made from ponderosa pine, homemade gesso, natural pigments, piñon sap varnish, and a beeswax coating; all bultos are made from cottonwood root, homemade gesso, natural pigments, piñon sap varnish, and a beeswax coating. The size and date of some pieces have been reconstructed from the artist's memory.

Library of Congress Catalog Card Number: 94-77890
ISBN 0-9641542-0-X

TABLE OF CONTENTS

ABOVE: Manger Scene retablo, 1978. Size: 16" x 9". Acrylic paint on a piece of scrap oak. One of the earliest pieces done by Charlie Carrillo. Artist's Collection. Photo by Robert Reck.

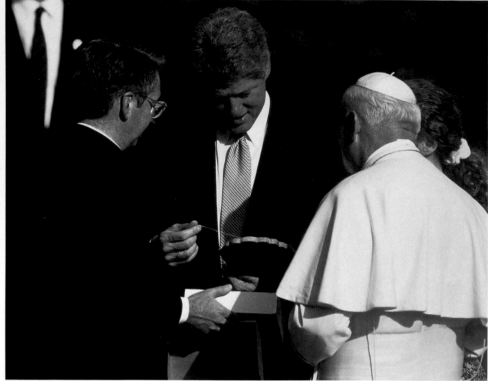

PREFACE

TOP LEFT: San Ignacio de Loyola retablo, 1988. Size: 7" x 10.5". Presented to President Bill Clinton by Regis University. Currently part of the President's Gift Collection, White House. Charlie modeled this retablo after an early piece by José Rafael Aragón. See William Wroth's *Christian Images in Hispanic New Mexico*, page 134, plate 97 and Robin Farwell Gavins' *Traditional Arts of Spanish New Mexico*, page 44. Photo by Father Thomas Steele, S.J.

TOP RIGHT: President Bill Clinton received a retablo by Charlie Carrillo from the Regis University Collection of New Mexican Santos during his visit with Pope John Paul II in 1993. Photo courtesy Barry Staver.

When we first started collecting Hispanic art we heard many stories about Charlie Carrillo. We formed a mental image of the santero based on those stories. We envisioned Charlie as a wise, old, holy man, possessing all of the accumulated knowledge of the Penitente movement. Many other people also have had similar images of Charlie.

We were startled to find out that Charlie wasn't yet forty years old, that he had started carving late in the nineteen seventies, and was still a dedicated student of Hispanic culture, the Penitentes, iconography and his religion. As we got to know Charlie better we also found him to be a warmhearted person who puts family first. He is especially proud of his wife Debbie's accomplishments in pottery and his children's interest in his art form. Charlie is constantly giving back to the community. If people express interest in the art form, Charlie will take time to educate them. A devout Catholic, Charlie is a down to earth real person.

This book was, for us, a labor of love. We are always among the many collectors and museums who vie for the limited number of Charlie's pieces at both the summer and winter Spanish Markets. We wrote this book so others could appreciate the range of Charlie's art as well as appreciate this unique art form. When we discovered contemporary Hispanic folk art, there really wasn't a lot written to answer all of our questions. Although santos appear all over the world as well as in other Hispanic countries, the New Mexican versions of the saints have a particular warmth and humanity that is like no other. The stories associated with each of the saints are also uniquely New Mexican.

We especially want to thank Charlie, Debbie, Estrellita, and Roán for their help and cooperation in putting together this book. We especially enjoyed Charlie and Debbie's meals, stories, and company. We made some great friends in the process of doing this book. When you look at many of the faces of San José or the male santos, you can't help but see Charlie.

One of the reasons Charlie is so popular right now is not just the beauty of his work. Charlie has educated and excited people about the stories and history of the santos. Although he could be producing more work, without the teaching and interaction the art form doesn't have the same impact and depth. Despite the fact that he may think of this book as "pouring gravy on his mashed potatoes," Charlie is delighted to share his art with a wider audience.

This book is by no means a scholarly piece in the traditional mold, although a lot of research has gone into producing it. It is also not an attempt by two "Anglos" to "wanna-be Hispanic." It is our love of the art form and the absence of things written on contemporary santeros that has driven us to write this book. We also realized about halfway through writing this book that if much more time had gone by, it would have been very difficult to track down the information and pieces. It has been important to have Charlie share some of these stories instead of trying to guess what he might have said.

Ownership credits when known at the time of publication are given with permission by the owner. We have made great efforts to try to find many of Charlie's significant pieces. The process of selling work in crowds sometimes means that records are not accurately kept. In some cases, photos taken by Charlie before pieces were sold have been used. We have made an attempt to share with you the most important and interesting of Charlie's work to date. We know that there are a lot more pieces of his work to be seen and apologize to anyone who feels their work should have been included. At the time of printing this book, Charlie had made over 3,500 pieces of art.

In researching this book, we studied over 1,200 pieces from 1977 to present. We saw three distinct phases in the development of his work — first there were acrylics of a very crude form (by today's standard) up until about 1980; then came a watercolor period with more refined lines in his work from 1980 to 1987; and finally, natural pigments on hand-adzed ponderosa pine beginning about 1987. We will probably see even more spectacular pieces as Charlie moves into what will be a fourth phase.

We also would like to thank: Diana Pardue of The Heard Museum; Linda Tyler of The Tamarind Institute; Ellen Landis of Albuquerque Museum; Robin Gavin of Museum of International Folk Art; Cynthia Nakamura and Inga Calvin of The Denver Art Museum; Laurie Beth Kalb of the Gene Autry Western Heritage Museum; Kathy Reynolds and Cathy Wright of the Taylor Museum of Southwestern Studies; Richard Ahlborn of the Smithsonian National Museum of American History; Father Chris Zugger of Our Lady of Perpetual Help Church, Albuquerque; Sister Lucy and Bishop Ricardo Ramírez, C.S.B. of the Diocese of Las Cruces; David Smoker; Kathy Hart; Rey Móntez; Janis Cromer; Ana Montoya; Mary Anne Isaac; Beverly Duran; Margaret Duran; Roseanne Aceves; Jim Liller of Checkmate Graphics Pre-Press; Bud Redding & Pat Price of the Spanish Colonial Arts Society; John Berkenfield & Felipe Mirabal of El Rancho de las Golondrinas; Father Thomas Steele, S.J.; Mary Ryland of the Archdiocese of Santa Fe; all the collectors who shared their pieces with us; the photographers who helped us make the pieces look their best; the other santeros who shared their insights with us — Nick, Alcario, David, Jerome, Jake, Ernie, Ramón, Irene, Victor, Jimmy and Debbie (to name just a few); and San Francisco de Sales, patron of writers and editors.

TOP: San José bulto, 1980. Size: 18" tall. Acrylic paint on cottonwood root; handmade turquoise and silver crown on both San Jóse and Niño. This was Charlie's first bulto; it sold at the 1980 Spanish Market. Private Collection. Photo by artist.

BOTTOM: Santa Barbara retablo, 1994. Size: 10" x 14". This retablo sold at the 1994 Spanish Market. Private Collection. Photo by Ron Behrmann.

We dedicate this book to our parents — Ruth, Jane, Bob, and Charles — who instilled in both of us a love of learning and a desire to be a part of a greater community.

We all will need to see what Charlie is doing ten years from now, but for now enjoy!

Barbe Awalt and Paul Rhetts

> "This is one of those art forms you cannot separate from the people. We write our own history by what we say and the art we do."
>
> Charlie Carrillo

TOP: Nuestra Señora de Guadalupe en Nicho, 1991. Size: 7" tall bulto; 8" tall nicho box. Charlie had been looking at nicho boxes at the Taylor Museum and realized that very few old nichos had survived. He found one made by Pedro Antonio Fresquís which had curtain pulls as a decorative element. After he made this box, he decided it needed a Guadalupana. He carved the angel and the Guadalupana out of one piece of wood, adding the rays separately. This is the smallest Guadalupana Charlie has ever made. Authors' Collection. Photo by Ron Behrmann.

FOREWORD/PRÓLOGO

El arte del santero ha sido primordial para el enriquecimiento de la cultura Hispana en Nuevo México por casi 400 años. De iglesias poblanas a capillas privadas a los moradas sagradas del la Hermandad Penitente, el trabajo individual del santero ha sido el de proveer a las generaciones de Nuevo Mexicanos con símbolos de inspiración de identidad y de fe, y de una esperanza colectiva para el futuro.

La importancia de dicho simbolismo en la cultura Hispana contemporánea ha sido reenforzada durante la última década con una reinsurgencia extraordinaria de artistas quienes escogen trabajar de acuerdo a la tradición del santero. Artistas jóvenes y viejos están virando hacia este arte espectacular de fe como forma de expresar orgullo y conocimiento de su herencia, y sobre todo, como forma de expresarsá a sí mismos. Al traer una perspectiva moderna a un arte antiguo, no solo están preservando una tradición histórica y espiritual importante, están infundiendo una nueva forma de vida.

Una figura singular en esta nueva generación de santeros es la de Charlie Carrillo, un hombre cuya reverencia hacia el arte y la historia detrás de ella ha elevado lo que una vez se consideró como forma de arte folklórico a una forma, métodos y materiales tradicionales Español-Colonial. Charlie se ha sometido a la investigación y experimentación extensiva, augmentando así conocimientos nuevos importantes de técnicas tradicionales muy valuables tanto para el estudiante (aprendíz) como para el maestro. Charlie ha empleado estas técnicas creando así su distinguido repertorio artístico. Con su pureza, simplicidad y refinamiento simultáneo, el trabajo de Charlie demuestra un nivel de calidad y excelencia reservado solamente para los maestros de la tradición del santero.

Pero más notable que la artesanía de Charlie es el espíritu que le da a su trabajo. Ya sea demostrando su arte a un salón lleno de niños, restaurando una morada, o alentando a un jóven santero alcazar su oficio, Charlie emana energía y entusiasmo ilimitado por su cultura. Esto es particularmente importante en un tiempo cuando muchos están reclamando que la cultura Hispana Nuevo-Mexicana ha sido olvidada. El ejemplo de Charlie, sin embargo, demuestra lo contrario; su cultura Hispana no está olvidada, esta floreciendo.

The art of the santero has been central to the sustenance of the Hispanic culture in New Mexico for nearly 400 years. From village churches to private chapels to the sacred moradas of the Penitente Brotherhood, the works of individual santeros have provided generations of New Mexicans with inspiring symbols of a shared identity and faith, and a collective hope for the future.

The importance of such symbolism in contemporary Hispanic culture has been reinforced during the past decade with an extraordinary resurgence of artists choosing to work in the santero tradition. Artists young and old are turning to this spectacular art of faith as a way to express pride and awareness in their heritage, and more importantly, as a way to express themselves. By bringing a modern perspective to an age-old art, they are not only preserving a historically and spiritually important tradition, they are infusing it with new life.

A key figure in this new generation of santeros is Charlie Carrillo, a man whose reverence for the art and the history behind it has helped elevate what was once considered a folk art form to a fine art form. As a staunch supporter of the use of traditional Spanish Colonial methods and materials, Charlie has undertaken extensive research and experimentation, gaining important new knowledge of traditional techniques that is valuable in the education of student and scholar alike. Then Charlie has put those techniques to use in creating his distinctive artistic repertoire. At once pure, simple, and highly refined, Charlie's work demonstrates a level of quality and excellence reserved only for the masters of the santero tradition.

But even more notable than Charlie's artistry is the spirit that he brings to his work. Whether demonstrating his art to a roomful of children, restoring a run-down morada, or encouraging a young santero to pursue the craft, Charlie exudes boundless energy and enthusiasm for his culture. This is particularly important at a time when many are claiming that New Mexico's Hispanic culture has been forgotten. Charlie's example, however, proves otherwise: the Hispanic culture is not forgotten, it is flourishing.

Carmella Padilla, Writer/Escritora, Santa Fe
Vice President, Spanish Colonial Arts Society

Levanté la tabla cortada a mano y la olí profundamente. Era el aroma del piñon fresco, una de las fragancias más maravillosas en su naturaleza, y provenía de una pieza de arte religiosa. Si hubiese un aroma y símbolo visual de Nuevo México, no podría haber casamiento más perfecto.

"¡Que le ha puesto a ésto!," pregunté, y el artista procedió a darme una receta, una lección de historia y una fe renovada en humanidad.

Había estudiado arte de joven y había aprendido, con gran frustración, la actitud tan protegida de muchos artistas hacia sus fórmulas que eran secretas para ellos, recetas clandestinas que se llevaban a la sepultura y ¿porque? ¿Acaso el arte, no es una interpretación individual después de todo? No son fórmulas solo un medio para un fin, y sinceramente, ¿algo para conpartirse con los creadores projimos? ¡Y aquí me encontraba yo, un extraño por completo, y este humilde y benevolente artista estaba compartiendo su conocimiento conmigo!

Algunos genios viven su arte. Se demuestra en su conducta, su filosofía, la forma como tratan a los demás, en lo que comen y beben, y en el caso de este artista, como y que cocinan — entrelazdo como el bouquet del piñon y el arte del santero. Para todos ustedes afortunados que conocen a Charlie, saben a que me refiero. Para los que no, es más de lo que uno puede formular en la imaginación. Es el tierno esposo y padre que rezo por llegar a ser cuando me case y tenga hijos; es el amigo fiel que espero ser yo; es un humilde artista, penitente y historiador que yo seré en mis sueños; y es el maestro benevolente que será recordado más allá cuando todos nos hayamos vuelto en el barro con que pinta — el mismo barro que alienta a los árboles de piñon y a nuestro querido Nuevo México.

No hay persona que haya tenido mas efecto en preservar los procesos tradicionales y en enseñarlos que mi amigo, Charles M. Carrillo. ¡Verdaderamente, es el maestro!

TOP: Roán Carrillo was caught among his father's work at 1988 Spanish Market. Photo by Fred Cisneros.

BOTTOM: Charlie paints a retablo in his studio, 1991. Photo by Ron Behrmann.

I picked up the hand-cut board and inhaled deeply. It was the aroma of fresh piñon, one of the most wonderful fragrances in nature, and it was coming from a masterpiece of religious art. If there were a scent and a visual symbol of New Mexico, they could not be more perfectly wedded.

"What did you put on this?" I asked, and the artist proceeded to give me a recipe, a history lesson, and a renewed faith in humanity.

I had studied art as a younger man and had known, with great frustration, the guarded attitude that many artists have with formulas that were secret to them, clandestine recipes which would go to their graves, and why? Isn't art always an individual interpretation, after all? Were not formulas only a means to that end and, truly, something to be shared with fellow creators? And here I was, a complete stranger, and this benevolent and humble artist was sharing all of his knowledge with me!

Some geniuses live their art. It's in their demeanor, their philosophy, how they treat others, what they eat and drink and, as in the case of this artist, how and what they cook – interwoven like the bouquet of piñon and santero art. For those of you fortunate enough to know Charlie, you know what I mean. For those of you who don't, he is more than you can conjure up in your imagination. He is the tender husband and father I pray I will be when I am married and have children; he is the loyal friend I hope I am; he is the unassuming artist, Penitente, and historian I shall be in my dreams; and he is the benevolent teacher that will be remembered long after we have all returned to the clay he paints with – the same clay that feeds the piñon trees of our beloved Nuevo México.

No single person has had a greater effect in preserving traditional processes and teaching them than my friend, Charles M. Carrillo. *Verdaderamente, es el maestro.*

Rey Móntez, Móntez Gallery

TOP: Charlie puts the finishing touches on his display of his San Isidro Labrador bulto at 1990 Spanish Market. This bulto received the Grand Prize Best of Show Award. Photo by Fred Cisneros.

BOTTOM: Charlie hurriedly works to get ready for Spanish Market, 1991. Photo by Ron Behrmann.

Lo que atrae a la gente hacia Charles Carrillo es su talento como artista, su conocimiento como erudito, su abilidad para transmitir ideas sobre la vida Hispana, la cultura y la história siente al conocerlo a el y a su familia. Su consejo es buscado bastamente por un gran número de museos por toda la nación, y Charles Carrillo siempre encuentra tiempo para crear arte entre la confusión del constante timbre del teléfono y de la puerta de repetidas peticiones de su tiempo, energía y pensamiento intelectual.

En la última parte de la década de los 80's, The Heard Museum comenzó a trabajar en asociación con el artista Charles Carrillo para dar forma a las actividades del museo en años por venir. Charles Carrillo, conocido como simplemente Charlie para amigos y colégas, fué inicialmente consejero y líder para un viaje a Santa Fe patrocinado por el museo. Alrededor del tiempo en que ocurrió el viaje, la administración del Museo comezaba a despertar interés en la colección de arte Hispano de Nuevo México.

La asociación entre el Museo y Charlie aumentó cuando el revisó y comentó sobre la colección Colonial-Española del Museo, y posteriormente sirvió como miembro del equipo de planeación de una exhibición contemporánea del arte Hispano de Nuevo México (¡Chispas!). En las primeras etapas de discusión, Charlie amplió la cuota de consejeros al incluir dos colégas: a Teresa Archuleta-Sagel y Luís Tapia. Cada uno al contribuir al desarrollo de la exhibición ¡Chispas! se convirtió en un esfuerzo colectivo entre artistas y el personal del museo.

Al estar trabajando en ¡Chispas!, Charlie revisó la colección del Museo sobre Santos de Nuevo México. A travéz de los esfuerzos de Charlie, el Museo amplió extensivamente sus conocimientos e información sobre esta colección. Mucho también fue aprendido acerca de los tejidos históricos por parte de Teresa Archuleta-Sagel y de los muebles

Colonial-Españoles de Luís Tapia. Además de la exhibición <u>¡Chispas!</u>, material histórico se mostró durante algunos meses en otra sección del Museo.

Lo que queda de <u>¡Chispas!</u> es un pequeño catálogo. Lo que permanece de la experiencia es una gran amistad y un respecto profundo hacia todos los artistas implicados, y la realización de que la exhibición se convirtió en lo que fué por la voluntad de Charlie al incluir los conocimientos colectivos de otros para formar la exposición.

What draws people to Charles Carrillo is his talent as an artist, his knowledge as a scholar, his ability to convey ideas about Hispanic life, culture, and history in New Mexico, and the immediate sense of friendship one experiences upon meeting him and his family. Widely sought for advice by a number of museums throughout the country, Charles Carrillo still finds the time to create art among the confusion of the constantly ringing phone and doorbell accompanied by repeated requests to give of his time, energy, and intellectual thought.

In the late 1980s, The Heard Museum began a working association with artist Charles Carrillo that would help shape the Museum's activities for the next several years. Charles Carrillo, known simply as Charlie to friends and colleagues, was initially an advisor and leader for a Museum-sponsored trip to Santa Fe. Around the time the trip occurred, the Museum staff was experiencing an awakened interest in its collection of Hispanic art from New Mexico.

The association between the Museum and Charlie broadened as he reviewed and commented on the Museum's Spanish Colonial collection and later served as a team member in the planning of a contemporary exhibit of Hispanic art of New Mexico (<u>¡Chispas!</u>). In the early stages of discussion, Charlie broadened the base of advisors to include two colleagues, Teresa Archuleta-Sagel and Luís Tapia. As each contributed to the exhibit's development, <u>¡Chispas!</u> became a collective effort between artists and Museum staff.

While working on <u>Chispas!</u>, Charlie reviewed the Museum's collection of New Mexico santos. Through Charlie's efforts, the Museum gained extensive information about its collection. Much was also learned about the historic textiles from Teresa Archuleta-Sagel and Spanish Colonial furniture from Luís Tapia. In addition to the <u>¡Chispas!</u> exhibit, historic material was displayed for a few months in another part of the Museum.

What is left of <u>¡Chispas!</u> is a small catalogue. What remains of the experience is a close friendship and deep regard for all of the artists involved and the realization that the exhibit became what it was through the willingness of Charlie to include the collective thoughts of others to shape the show.

Diana Pardue, Curator of Collections/Curador de Colecciones,
The Heard Museum

En 1988, mi amigo Ray Dewey insistió en que conociera al prominente santero e historeador Charlie Carrillo. Para mi placer, descubrí a un hombre con un sentido de la história sin igual. Y descubrí a una persona a quién podría respetar como artista.

Charlie aporta integridad y una fuerza creativa a un campo que a veces queda destituido como un arte menor. Por medio de su investigación tan diligente y cuidadoso trabajo, Charlie ha mejorado ese campo. Su inclinación por la investigación histórica lo ha llevado a re-decubrir, re-indentificar y a fabricar las pinturas y barnices antiguos que fueron usados por sus antepasados. Este esfuerzo pionero ha afectado enormemente a otros escultores y ha producido un florecimiento de imitadores.

TOP: Charlie tells the stories behind the santos at 1988 Spanish Market. Charlie's Hispanic Heritage Award for in-depth research is hanging on the back wall of his booth. Photo by Fred Cisneros.

BOTTOM: Charlie works on a bulto in his studio, 1991. Photo by Ron Behrmann.

> **"The crucifix is the essence of all the stories — it has so much of the teachings of the morada."**
>
> Charlie Carrillo

Charlie es un inovador. No solo su investigación en la pintura ha sentado precedente, sino que continua conceptualmente a abrir paso a nuevos caminos. Entre tres o cuatro "líderes" en este campo, continuamente sale con conceptos nuevos y los ejecuta magistralmente. Tiene un excelente sentido de línea y su abilidad para el dibujo seguidamente lo mantiene aparte de sus iguales. Todo ésto es dentro de los márgenes de una estructura de trabajo histórica a los cuales se apega, sin embargo, constantemente por expanderlos.

Mi amistad con Charlie es de un espíritu afín, una asociación muy agradable. La pegadura que nos une es una mentalidad del período Post-Gótico, una visión como la del Siglo XIV para ver al mundo. No hay muchas personas con esta actitud. Ambos somos de la misma longitud de onda — ambos surgimos del mundo del Rey Felipe El Huero, repleto de Hieronymus Bosch, Albrecht Durer, Lucas Cranach y de los hermanos Van Eyck. Ambos tenemos un fuerte lazo con la historia. Utilizamos a la historia como base para nuestras declaraciones visuales. Yo no tengo muchos amigos que sean artistas porque, aunque extraño, tenemos poco en común. Charlie, sin embargo, verdaderamente tiene algo que decir y muy serio con lo que hace. El exhibe amor por su arte.

Charlie está en un punto de su carrera que puede hacer lo que quiera. Puede continuar a expander su imaginación. O puede continuar a producir extensas y más complicadas piezas — inclusive expander a más y diferentes fuentes de comunicación.

In 1988 my friend Ray Dewey insisted that I meet the prominent santero and historian Charlie Carrillo. To my delight, I discovered a man with outrageous humor and someone whose knowledge and sense of history is without parallel. And,I found a person whom I could respect as an artist.

Charlie brings integrity and a creative force to a field sometimes dismissed as a minor art. By his diligent research and careful work, Charlie has elevated that field. His penchant for historical research has led him to rediscover, reidentify, and manufacture the old paints and varnishes which were used by his ancestors. This pioneering effort has greatly affected other carvers and has produced a flourish of imitators.

Charlie is an innovator. Not only has his paint research taken hold, but he continues to blaze new trails conceptually. Among three or four "leaders" in the field, he continuously comes up with new concepts and masterfully executes them. He has an excellent sense of line and his drawing ability often sets him apart from his peers. All of this is within the confines of an historic framework to which he adheres but which he constantly labors to expand.

My friendship with Charlie is one of a kindred spirit, a pleasant association. The glue that binds us is a post-Gothic mind set — a 14th/15th Century view of the world. Not many people have this attitude. We are both on the same wavelength — we were both sprung from the world of King Philip the Fair, filled with Hieronymus Bosch, Albrecht Durer, Lucas Cranach and the van Eyck brothers. We both have a very serious tie to history. We use history as a base for our visual statements. I don't have a lot of artist friends because, strangely enough, we have little in common. Charlie, however, actually has something to say and he is serious about what he does. He exhibits a love for his art.

Charlie is at a point in his career where he can do anything he wants. He can continue to expand the imagery. Or he can go on to produce larger, more complicated pieces — even branching out into more and different media.

TOP: Rosalia de Palermo retablo, 1994. Size: 11" x 13.5". Private Collection. Photo by Ron Behrmann.

Paul Pletka, Artist/Artista

INTRODUCTION

What is a Santero?

A great deal of the controversy around "being a santero" is a problem of time. The santeros of old New Mexico made a living creating saints for personal and group worship. They were artisans as well as teachers. By their travels they were also a primary reason why stories were shared from community to community. The stories traveled freely from Mexico to New Mexico, many times originating in Central and South America and even in Europe. The santos made in New Mexico "not only serve their intended roles as instruments that provide devotional 'windows' to the divine, but also as devices for maintaining a cultural identity." But surprisingly, these same santos, Charlie believes, are devices that help enculturate "outsiders" and give them a more balanced notion of New Mexican history, social values, moral beliefs, religious devotion, art, and even geography.

The Catholic church and its missionaries arrived in New Mexico in the late 16th Century along with the Spanish Conquistadores. The missionaries stayed on to establish missions among the people. New Mexico was a rough terrain, bringing many hardships to the residents. The religious art in the region was, according to Mitchell Wilder, "tucked away in a time capsule – nicely insulated against foreign influences, in a sort of cultural hypnosis."

Many purists say that a true santero should spread the word and art in the old way. But frankly, if the old santeros had had cars for transportation or mass media to spread the word, they would have used them. The santeros of old were products of the culture at that

ABOVE: Charlie and Debbie Carrillo gave a retablo to Queen Sophia and King Juan Carlos of Spain during their visit to New Mexico in 1987 prior to the opening of the Hispanic Heritage Wing, Museum of International Folk Art, Santa Fe. When he was approached by the Museum of International Folk Art to do a piece for the King of Spain, Charlie wanted to give back to the people of Spain something in thanks for what they gave the people of New Mexico. Photo courtesy Office of the Governor, New Mexico.

TOP: *Adán y Eva/Adam and Eve retablo, 1991. Size: 12" x 25". God the Father is watching over Adam and Eve. Private Collection. Photo by Craig Varjabedian.*

BOTTOM: *Santo Niño de Atocha retablo, 1988. Size: 8" x 11". Collection of Jennifer Martinez and William McArthur. Photo by Robert Reck.*

time in history, and contemporary santeros are also a product of all the complications of our current culture. Purists will criticize a Santo Niño wearing blue jeans and flannel when in fact, the old santos wore clothing of the times. Throughout history, santeros were only males. Today the tradition is carried on by men, women, and even children. Traditional Spanish Colonial art can also mistakenly get caught up in the "Santa Fe Style" feeding frenzy that makes the santos more a fetish than an object of devotion.

But being a santero in the strictest interpretation is not just teaching, sharing and making art, it is also a way of life. According to Charlie's close friend Father Tom Steele, "Santeros are now the driving force, passing along the traditions — working with others. They pass along the oral traditions, the ways of life, and 'why we live the way we live'." In the villages of old New Mexico the oral history only had to circulate among the immediate population, since isolation was a constant factor. In contemporary New Mexico, students travel from as far away as Japan to hear the stories and collect the santos. The retablos originally had to be made because the paintings from Spain were few and far between. The isolation of the New Mexican villages dictated a unique art form that grew and changed through time with limited outside contact.

But it is what Charlie calls the "belief system" that brings you to the essence of the santero. "If I didn't truly believe in it, I couldn't do it. If you don't believe, you are just a painter of images." The "it" is the religion, not necessarily an organized, group activity but the oneness with the images and their story. Charlie calls it collapsing history so that when he paints or carves a saint, he is in the scene — talking to the saints, seeing the story in first person. It is this personal identification that links Charlie with the Native Americans who see the kachinas from the kivas as real beings who have an impact on lives. The santos don't become objects of devotion until they are blessed by a priest. But as Charlie works on the santos they are personal friends.

To Charlie, the iconography of the santos is one of the most important factors. They tell the stories in often very subtle ways. Although he has been called a cultural warrior he is more like a culture broker. The research of the saints, their stories and the attached iconography is of primary importance to Charlie in the creative process. You simply don't paint a robe your favorite color or put a flower on a retablo because it looks nice. There is a science of numbers, 3s, 5s, 7s, 12s. Seven sorrows, ten commandments, fourteen stations of the cross, the tiny details in the pictures all go back to the numbers and their important events in the stories. Everything has a meaning.

Charlie will become quite demonstrative about the controversy — are santeros of today folk artists? He says "Don't folk me up!" According to Charlie, Hispanic religious art of New Mexico is really *arte sagrada* (sacred art), not just another regional folk art. He feels that santos are fine art and to categorize them as folk art is an academic put-down. Again, the comparison to Hopi kachinas is the same. Kachinas are not viewed by their makers as a folk craft but as an extension of religious beliefs.

Charlie has also researched the santeros of New Mexico until they have become so familiar that they are his friends. He recognizes their color symbolism and artistic styles. Father Steele claims that if Charlie were asked to draw up a psychological profile of José Raphael Aragón, Molleno, or any of the historic santeros, that they would be surprisingly accurate — if anyone could claim to have known them. To see Charlie enter the collections of a museum and start rattling on about examples is truly a wondrous experience. He often points out to astonished museum curators that items are identified incorrectly and will carefully point out each characteristic to prove the point. After a lesson, it is so simply clear to even the untrained eye.

It is often asked if Charlie is a holy man since he is a santero. Having the title of santero doesn't automatically convey sainthood. A santero isn't necessarily better than any other person, but a santero does have more contact with the stories of good conquering evil and salvation. And by virtue of the fact that a santero spends a great deal of time in solitary contemplation of the saints and their stories, a santero has the opportunity to be the same positive force in the community today that the first santeros were in early New Mexico.

All this rationalization, however, doesn't explain the numbers of people who flock to Charlie's lectures and exhibits. It is beyond simple artistic adulation; they need to hear what he says. Are they looking for something lacking in their modern lives? Does Charlie know something the rest of the world doesn't yet know? Is there a reason why other santeros have to study with Charlie to learn his secrets and techniques? Whatever the answer is, Charlie Carrillo has an impact and effect on people in many different ways. Not only does his art speak, but he speaks in a profound way to the people. Charlie Carrillo is a santero of modern New Mexico.

TOP: King Juan Carlos and Queen Sophia of Spain inspect the retablo from Charlie Carrillo during their visit to New Mexico in 1987 prior to the opening of the Hispanic Heritage Wing at the Museum of International Folk Art in Santa Fe. Photo courtesy of the Office of the Governor, New Mexico.

LEFT: Fe de Nuestros Antepasados/ Faith of Our Ancestors retablo, 1987. Size: 14" x 24". A gift to King Juan Carlos and Queen Sophia of Spain, the retablo shows the three devotions – Saint Francis for the Franciscan missionaries who colonized the New World; Saint Teresa de Avila, a mystic from Spain, who represents devotion and woman's contribution to the New World; and San Isidro, from Madrid, who represented the agricultural tradition in the New World. Photo by the artist.

ABOVE: Debbie Carrillo gives her grandmother Belen Trujillo a hug. The altar screen/reredos from the Morada del Alto at Abiquiú is in the background. The altar screen was destroyed in the 1992 fire at Abiquiú morada. Photo by Neil Jacobs, *Albuquerque Journal* "Sage," December 2, 1990.

RIGHT: Charlie poses with San Rafael en Nicho/Saint Rafael bulto, 1992. Size: 23.5" tall. Exhibited as a part of the Albuquerque Museum *Charles M. Carrillo: Santos* show in 1993 to celebrate "The Year of American Craft: A Celebration of the Creative Work of the Hand." Private Collection. Photo by Robert Reck.

"I come from a family
of teachers of culture."
Charlie Carrillo

THE SANTERO

Charles M. Carrillo was not born to an established woodcarving family but to a family of school teachers in Albuquerque, New Mexico, in 1956. Charlie, his twin brother Andy, brothers Tony and David, and sister Cathy, were born to Dr. Rafael A. and Loretta Torres Carrillo. His grandmother, Edna Torres, is given credit by Charlie as always keeping him interested in drawing, beginning as a very young child. She was bedridden and, when her medicine was delivered, there were always coloring books or crayons in the order. Charlie considered himself to be a very fortunate child always to have this luxury. Dr. and Mrs. Carrillo can trace their family back to settlers who came to New Mexico in the 1690s and to Genízaros and Native Americans from the New Mexican Pueblos.

Charlie graduated from Manzano High School in Albuquerque and went on to receive an undergraduate degree in Anthropology from the University of New Mexico. He envisioned for himself a life of teaching and archaeological research. The process continued with a Masters Degree in Anthropology from the University of New Mexico in 1983, and currently Charlie is a doctoral candidate at the University of New Mexico. His area of expertise in the academic world is not santos nor the religious heritage of New Mexico, but historic archaeology and, most especially, Colonial New Mexico Hispanic ceramic traditions. As a contract archeologist for the University of New Mexico, Charlie prepared reports on the acequias of El Llano, testing and analysis of two Mountain Bell sites in Corrales, and the Abiquiú Reservoir Project for the Army Corps of Engineers.

But it was during the work in Abiquiú that Charlie's life changed in many lasting ways. In 1977 Charlie was hired by the community of Abiquiú to direct the archeological program at La Capilla de Santa Rosa de Lima site (the first Spanish settlement in the northern Chama River valley) and to oversee a summer program for high school students. During that period, Charlie was introduced by one of his employees to Debbie Barbara

TOP RIGHT: Nuestra Señora de los Dolores bulto patiently waits for a sale at 1989 Spanish Market. Photo by Fred Cisneros.

TOP LEFT: Adán y Eva/Adam and Eve retablo, 1991. Size: 22" x 16". Typically Charlie's pieces are made with the wood grain going vertically. This piece, however, was done with the grain in a horizontal direction. José Rafael Aragón did a similar tableau of Adam and Eve; see William Wroth's Christian Images in Hispanic New Mexico, plate 103. Private Collection. Photo by Craig Varjabedian.

TOP: Nuestra Señora de Guadalupe retablo, 1992. Size: 8" x 16". Private Collection. Photo by Ron Behrmann.

BOTTOM: Award-winning retablo of Nuestra Señora de Guadalupe by Estrellita de Atocha Carrillo, age 8, 1989 Spanish Market. Size: 11" x 15.5". Collection of Keith and Letta Wofford. Photo by Robert Reck.

Eliza Trujillo. In 1978 Charlie and Debbie were married in Abiquiú, where Debbie's family has lived since the 1700s.

Charlie was getting deeply immersed in the cultural heritage of Abiquiú and of the people of Northern New Mexico. His dream was to try to set up a cultural center for the community and revive the arts and crafts of the people. Although he never paid a lot of attention to the images of the saints/santos while he was growing up, he knew they were always around. Artist Paul Pletka maintains that whatever children experience between the ages of 6 and 14 will influence their development and art for the rest of their lives.

Charlie was introduced to the Morada at Abiquiú and to the Penitente Brotherhood of Our Father Jesus the Nazarene (Los Hermanos). The images now took on greater meaning to Charlie, the traditional arts of the Spanish Colonial period now were alive and no longer just in a textbook. Charlie began to make a few santos in 1977. In 1978 a few more were made and he was hooked.

Through the efforts of his wife's cousin Dexter Trujillo, Charlie approached the Brotherhood and asked if he could become an apprentice. The Morada at Abiquiú had seen its membership grow old, and the elder brothers were no longer able to teach to a new generation or to keep up the place of worship, so he apprenticed for one year. After a year of learning at the Coyote Morada, it was hoped that Charlie and more young men would continue the age-old practices. During the apprenticeship, Charlie visited many moradas and saw old and beautiful bultos and retablos "that made him salivate." He began to research their history and meaning to the Brotherhood.

Charlie's first participation in the annual July Spanish Market in Santa Fe was in 1980 with approximately 40 other artists and two-month-old Estrellita de Atocha Carrillo. At the end of Market, Charlie had sold all of his retablos for a total of $714. He had brought some 16 retablos and a small altar screen. "We never had that much extra money in our lives," explains Debbie. It was the beginning of a career that would, at first, supplement the minimum wages paid to a contract archeologist/graduate student. Charlie initially thought of his career as an archeology professor, then later realized that his calling had a much wider appeal as an artist and lecturer on the Hispanic tradition in New Mexico. At his first Spanish Market, Charlie and Debbie became close to Jane Hall of Santa Fe. They call her "The Angel in Blue Jeans." Ms. Hall told Charlie, "This is what you will be doing for the rest of your life." At the time, Debbie and Charlie couldn't imagine it, but it has now proven to be true. Jane Hall also helped Charlie with graduate school through a scholarship and other support. He will never forget her help.

Charlie can now laugh about a few of his early pieces. He still has a few of the early retablos on rough board, painted in acrylics. One of his first big sales was a "funky/folk altar with tin and all sorts of other stuff nailed to it." That piece brought $400. According to Debbie, "It was the largest check we had ever gotten for one piece of art. We were struggling at the time – working at the University for a terribly low salary." Early works by Charlie used many different, traditional techniques like straw applique. And many collectors will be surprised that an early second place winning piece was a "Death Cart" at the Santa Fe Festival of the Arts in 1981.

As he studied for the Brotherhood, Charlie also did more research on the techniques used by early santeros. He studied not only the woods, colors, and pigments, but the meanings behind the pictures and the symbols used. A color like Prussian blue that early santeros used can only be gathered in the Zuni mountains from deposits of blue azurite. This color was described as early as 1604 and again in 1776 by Fray Francisco Atanasio Dominguez. Charlie has permission from the pueblo's elders to gather the crystals. A cave, that took him years to find in Questa, is the source of red oxide. For yellow ochre, Charlie travels near the Jicarilla Apache Reservation. Another source of this yellow earthen color is high up in the Sandia Mountains. He also finds yellow ochre near Regina. Dark brown is made by boiling the shells of black walnuts, while black comes from carbon soot. He celebrated a truly realistic flesh tone by giving jelly-jar containers of this pigment to fellow santeros at Christmas one year. He was hoping that they would use it, love it, and attempt the time-consuming task of making it from scratch from his recipe. One of Charlie's greens comes from a mineral deposit in the Placitas area. Indigo is only obtained from one Mexican family at $90-$300 a pound. The white background gesso is made from gypsum mined near Ghost Ranch which is close to Abiquiú. The gesso is mixed with a binder of animal-hide glue that Charlie processes. After completing a work, Charlie covers the piece with a homemade piñon sap varnish and a coat of beeswax.

The wood Charlie likes to use for bultos is cottonwood root that is no longer easy to find. "Before the damn dams along the Rio Grande, my ancestors would go down after a flood and find roots that had been torn up. Now, it is very difficult to find trees that have been uprooted." Retablos are made from hand-adzed ponderosa pine. He was given a piece of jelutong, a block of Indonesian wood, as a gift from friend and pupil Alcario Otero. Charlie is experimenting with it to see if it will act as a substitute for cottonwood root. Although it carves nicely, he says that it has a tendency to splinter.

The Family

The family unit and the extended family are an important part of Hispanic Northern New Mexico. The family elders pass the oral family history, including the stories of the saints down through the generations. For a long time this tradition, like the oral history in many other cultures, was in danger of being lost. Children did not want to grow up to be Hispanic. They wanted to be like the kids they saw on TV in the 1950s – white and middle class. You never saw a santero on TV, or for that matter a Hispanic. But a new pride in the traditions and heritage of the Hispanic people of New Mexico led to making sure the traditional ways did not die. Many of the old arts were "re-discovered" and the reasons why they were done in a certain way were studied.

The Carrillo family is very proud of their heritage. According to Debbie, her grandmother, Belen V. Trujillo, was the true artist. A weaver, a quilter, and a painter, she taught Debbie the art of ramilletes, paper flower making. Debbie tried a number of things without the inner feeling of success. "Charlie had more faith in me than I did." At Charlie's insistence, she studied under Felipe Ortega, a master potter of Hispanic and Jicarilla descent, and now is an accomplished potter of micaceous clay. They have at their home pots of the same type used in everyday cooking that have been passed down through the family. Debbie is now helped by the support of her own mother, especially when she needs to find the time to do her art with a busy family.

Roán and Estrellita have already started to make their mark on Spanish Market. Both have won first place ribbons in the children's division in different years. And both have been featured in the exhibit "Across Generations" at the Museum of International Folk Art and at a museum in Pueblo, Colorado. At the ripe old age of six, Estrellita was featured in a newspaper article on Spanish Market and how she had sold out of pieces within the first hour. That was hours before her father. Now, it is a race to see who will sell out first. The children are collectors of their patron saints – Estrellita with the Santo Niño de Atocha and Roán with San Miguel. They know the stories, the santeros and the various arts.

Debbie's Uncle Floyd Trujillo, taught by his father José C. Trujillo, was encouraged to exhibit "Shepherd's Ivory" by Charlie. Floyd came up with the term, also called bone carving. At first it was not allowed into the traditional arts of the Spanish Market. But Charlie took it as a challenge and researched the history, and found that bone carving

"If I die tomorrow I hope people remember the work I taught them. If you don't share knowledge it goes to the grave with you."

Charlie Carrillo

TOP: San Miguel Arcángel/Saint Michael the Archangel retablo, 1978. Size: 9" x 18". Acrylic paint on a rough-hewn log. This, a very early piece, was given to his parents. Charlie wanted to do a piece that contained his patron saint. This retablo is modeled after the work of Bernardo Miera y Pacheco in the San Miguel chapel in Santa Fe. See E. Boyd's *Popular Arts of Spanish New Mexico*, page 91, Figure 74. Artist's Collection. Photo by Robert Reck.

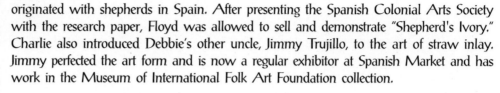

> ## "It is such a different art form – I have never had so much fun!"
> ### Charlie Carrillo

originated with shepherds in Spain. After presenting the Spanish Colonial Arts Society with the research paper, Floyd was allowed to sell and demonstrate "Shepherd's Ivory." Charlie also introduced Debbie's other uncle, Jimmy Trujillo, to the art of straw inlay. Jimmy perfected the art form and is now a regular exhibitor at Spanish Market and has work in the Museum of International Folk Art Foundation collection.

The Penitentes

In the late 1700s the Roman Catholic Penitente Brotherhood began in Northern New Mexico and Southern Colorado. Its beginnings were in response to a shortage of ordained clergy to minister to the needs of a very isolated and spread-out population. In the 19th Century, the traditions changed over time to a truly New Mexican style of devotion. The "Penitentes," as they are called today, are dedicated to a life of good while living a life of devotion to the suffering and death of Jesus Christ. During Holy Week, the "hermanos," or Brothers, pray the stations of the cross, recite the rosary, and engage in various forms of penance. Hymns of praise or "Alabados" are sung during many Holy Week processions and other religious activities throughout the year.

The Brothers meet in "moradas," simple buildings that serve as places of worship. Different rooms are used for eating and storage, while others are used for praying and devotion to the saints. Part of the duties of the Brothers is to care for the needy of the community and to continue to keep the traditions alive in the young. In modern times, the

TOP: Micaceous bean pot by Debbie Carrillo, 1992. Collection of Keith and Letta Wofford. Photo by Barbe Awalt.

BOTTOM: Farol/Spanish Colonial Lantern, 1988. Size: 7" x 10". Ponderosa pine, gypsum, and hide glue. Based on a picture in E. Boyd's Popular Arts of Spanish New Mexico, page 257, Figure 157. Private Collection. Photo by Ron Behrmann.

An Introduction to Terms

The art tradition of Northern New Mexico dates back to two major influences, the indigenous peoples – Native Americans and the first Spanish settlers who arrived in 1598. The arts were influenced by new products that were brought in by traders and the exposure to the rich traditional crafts and techniques, especially those of the Pueblo Indians of the Rio Grande Valley. This makes the arts of New Mexico a distinctive American form of expression with its own terminology.

A "santo" is a Spanish word for image of a saint or of a biblical event. There were santos in medieval Europe as well as the Philippines, South and Central America. The santos of New Mexico are unique in their stories and symbolism. The various santos are used in home devotion or in religious ceremonies. Many santos have handcrafted outfits for different times of the year.

A male "santero" or female "santera" is a person who creates images of saints.

A "retablo" is a two-dimensional painting of a saint or biblical event. In New Mexico the painting is usually done on a wood plank of ponderosa pine. In Mexico the paintings were made on tin. The retablo can hang by itself or in groupings on a wall, or it may be part of an altar screen.

A "bulto" is a three-dimensional painted sculpture of a saint or biblical scene. Its size can vary from miniature to life size for church use. The wood of choice is cottonwood root, but other woods may be used.

A "Reredos" ("altares" or "colaterales") is an altar screen with an architectural framework that has inserts of different saints. May be used in a private home chapel or a church. (French origin)

"Gesso" is used to cover the surface and give it a smooth surface to paint on. The homemade white coating is made from ground-up, baked anhydrated gypsum with a binder like glue made from animal skins.

"Penitente" is the common term used for members of the Penitente Brotherhood or more correctly "La Piadosa Fraternidad de Nuestro Padre Jesús Nazareno." This order of laymen who have been trained by elders uphold the Catholic New Mexican traditions of worship.

"Morada" is the chapel used by the Penitentes for worship. It is usually not open to the public and is usually in remote places in Northern New Mexico.

"Genízaro" culture of New Mexico is the mixture of Native American and Hispanic heritage. Genízaros were de-tribalized Hispanicized Indians. These peoples became part of the Hispanic culture of New Mexico and have greatly influenced the art forms and cultural milieu of New Mexico. Abiquiú was one of the largest Genízaro communities of the 18th Century, while other genízaros were found in Belen and Tomé, New Mexico.

Other Hispanic Folk Arts

Straw Inlay or Applique - The most common form is cut straw or corn husk applied to dark crosses then covered with a piñon sap varnish.

Weaving - "Saltillo, Serape & Rio Grande" blankets are still made today and are prized by collectors.

Colcha Embroidery - Wool on wool and wool on cotton embroidered coverlets, bedspreads, or altar frontals with intricate and colorful designs.

Ramilletes - Cut paper flowers used to decorate during festive or religious celebrations.

Jewelry - Sterling silver primarily was used for self adornment, tableware and occasionally on equestrian gear. Gold filagree, mined near Santa Fe, was very popular.

Tin Work - Punched and embossed tin used to decorate altars and religious items as well as for frames for mirrors and retablos and for boxes.

Furniture - Hand-carved territorial and Spanish Colonial furniture is still a part of the "Santa Fe" look. Cabinets, chests, trasteros, tables, and chairs were most popular.

Shepherd's Ivory - Bones from farm or local animals carved into small jewelry and utilitarian objects.

Leatherwork - Saddles, horse gear, coats, jackets, leggings, shoes, chests, and personal items were made in the Mexican and Spanish tradition.

Ironwork - The newly introduced horses and mules needed shoes and the firearms needed maintenance. Later decorative window treatments were introduced for security.

Architecture - The use of Native Pueblo, Spanish, Mexican and Southwest designs with local building materials resulted in Pueblo, Territorial, Colonial and New Mexican style houses of adobe brick. Wood "vigas," latillas, pillars, and carved doors are characteristic.

Micaceous Pottery - Ceramics made for everyday use with native clay containing mica. The fired pottery is a beautiful golden-copper color.

Hide Painting - Brain-tanned hides were used as canvas for religious paintings. These early santos were used by Franciscans to tell biblical stories and the lives of santos.

TOP: Adán y Eva/Adam and Eve retablo, 1990-91. Size: 20.5" x 32". Center from the serpent's head (Satan), the central trunk of the tree turns into Cristo Crucificado. A small dove is carved into the center of the crown at the top. Clockwise from upper left: God creates Adam; God creates Eve from Adam's rib; God gives Eve a sheep (a weaving) and Adam a sheath of wheat; San Miguel expels Adam and Eve from Paradise or the Garden. Collection of Michael and Ann Reynolds. Photo by Craig Varjabedian.

LEFT: Award-winning bulto of San Francisco de Asís by Roán Miguel Carrillo, age 8, 1993 Spanish Market. Size: 14" tall. Artist's Collection. Photo by Robert Reck.

✝

"The small town tradition has been acclimated by Charlie to today's life in contemporary times — taking the word to the people using today's media."

Thomas Steele, S.J.

TOP LEFT: San José Patriarca retablo, 1987. Size: 5.5" x 9". Regis University Collection of New Mexican Santos, Denver. Photo by Thomas Steele, S.J.

TOP RIGHT: San Francisco de Asís retablo by Roán Miguel Carrillo, age 6, 1991. Size: 6.5" x 12". Regis University Collection of New Mexican Santos, Denver. Photo by Thomas Steele, S.J.

BOTTOM: San José Patriarca retablo by Estrellita de Atocha Carrillo, age 7, 1987. Size: 6" x 9". Regis University Collection of New Mexican Santos, Denver. Photo by Thomas Steele, S.J.

Penitentes may be state employees, farmers, teenagers, retirees, and an unusually high number of artists. They meet usually once a month and each Friday during Lent and the last three days of Holy Week (Wednesday, Thursday, and Friday). They are hermanos for life.

Charlie belongs to La Morada de Nuestra Señora de Dolores del Alto de Abiquiú, the second oldest morada in New Mexico, built sometime between 1820 and 1850. It was the subject of one of Georgia O'Keefe's paintings. She was a resident of Abiquiú and lived a stone's throw away from the original morada. The three-room morada was vandalized and burned on September 17, 1992. It was a senseless act that brought the Penitentes to the front page and galvanized the Northern New Mexico communities to help rebuild. It also brought to the surface the fears of persecution. In addition to the damage, satanic symbols were painted on the ruins. Charlie, as hermano apostol of the brotherhood represents several Northern New Mexico moradas and felt obligated to help lead the restoration of the burned morada in Abiquiú. He was aided by fellow Brother Dexter Trujillo.

The Kit Carson Historical Museum in Taos donated thirty four items for the rebuilt morada, including two large and two small processional crosses, fourteen crosses for the stations of the cross, clothing for santos, and altar cloths. The items were acquired in the 1970s along with the Taos morada. The morada is not used by the Penitentes and is a part of the Museum facilities.

The fire was responsible for the loss of the building as well as many of the religious objects. One of the objects burned was an altar screen that was made by Charlie. He attributes the repatriation of the holy materials from the Kit Carson to the intervention of Rudy Herrera. Herrera, an employee of El Rancho de las Golondrinas, helped Charlie and the Kit Carson to start talking about the possibility of returning the materials to the Brotherhood. Adobe builder Albert Parra, donating his expertise and crew, was a driving force in the rebuilding of the morada. Albert is now the newest member of the Abiquiú morada. The Spanish Colonial Arts Society, with guidance from Sam Baca of the New Mexico Community Foundation, immediately threw support to the rebuilding process. Over $30,000 as well as many building materials were donated to the Brotherhood to rebuild the morada. A commemorative poster was designed by artist Lindsay Holt II and many local businesses donated materials, workmen, and supplies. Fearing that the vandals would return (they have never been caught), a state-of-the-art alarm system was installed. All of these changes were not welcomed by some of the older Hermanos from other moradas. But it was reasoned that the members would have built a place of worship that was consistent with the building methods of the day. The ruins were blessed and the new building rededicated just before Holy Week, 1993. Other unwelcome changes were the public discussions in the media of what the Penitentes do and what religious practices are followed. Although some limited information has come out, the traditions are still private and will remain that way.

Charlie still has items from the morada in his studio to restore, and he hopes that eventually others will turn up. Charlie and his friends are on the lookout at shops and at auctions for the other pieces that are still missing. More than seven months of santo making was put aside as Charlie set adobes and helped put the morada back together with the help of many volunteers. Although the vandalism was horrible, the community response to the rebuilding was a positive chapter and helped the public understand the role of the Penitentes in Northern New Mexico.

TOP: San Francisco retablo, 1980. Size: 9" x 14.5". Acrylic paint on commercial plank. Artist's Collection. Photo by Robert Reck.

BOTTOM: San Isidro Labrador retablo, 1991. Size: 17" x 23". Collection of David and Deborah Berardinelli. Photo by Ron Behrmann.

The Students

Charlie takes great pleasure in teaching. He takes valuable time from his schedule of making santos to lecture large numbers of groups. Many of these talks are for no pay or compensation but merely for the joy of sharing the traditions. The groups are often school children.

Charlie will talk very fondly of "the most influential person in my life as an educator – Powell Boyd." He says whenever he is creating a piece, at some point in the process, Powell Boyd will come into his mind. Mr. Boyd was the godfather of Charlie's twin brother Andy. As children, they were taught the Catholic stories of the saints by this man of many languages. As a teacher, Powell Boyd brought to Charlie a love of knowledge.

Because of Charlie's reputation for time-consuming research on pigments, symbolism, stories, and techniques, many beginning carvers, as well as established santeros, join him in his studio to talk and learn. Estrellita and Roán have always had other carvers and painters around the house.

When you talk to any of Charlie's "students" you begin to understand a lot about Charlie. Charlie gives a lot of himself to help his "students" find their own way. Just talk to Jake Serna, for example. Jake notes that he "never dreamed that I would be doing this. I have a calling to get back to my roots and my own personal faith. I am trying to find out what it is all about and why it is that way. My search had such a profound impact and it has led me to decide to do this full time. Art is an expression made up of feelings and emotions. My primary feeling is one of faith. I have explored my faith by looking at the santos of the great masters and by studying the new masters and learning from them. Also by really getting into my faith and prayers and alabados (prayer songs) and expressions that are drawn from faith. This all coalesced when I joined the morada." When he talks about Charlie the teacher, Jake says "*Semos cortado de mismo masa* – We are cut from the same dough."

There is controversy, though, about Charlie and his ideas. Some santeros feel threatened by the emphasis on technique, authenticity, and use of natural pigments. Some santeros also react poorly to the large number of Charlie's "students" who are now exhibiting and selling at Spanish Market. They long for the days of few exhibitors. But as Charlie sees it, "There are more people interested in Hispanic art and there is more of a market today. The good work continues to sell and command the highest prices." Many people ask if the relatively low prices for Hispanic art are now going to keep pace with Native American and contemporary art seen all over Santa Fe. Spanish Market is now a major event on the scale of Indian Market. Many Hispanics express happiness about the long-overdue respect that their art is now receiving, and many attribute that to Charlie and to other santeros like Ramón José López, Victor Goler, Felix López, Anita Romero Jones, and Marie Cash.

Charlie will continue to explore new designs, ideas and media. He was one of a group of santeros who were invited to make a portfolio of prints for the University of New Mexico's Tamarind Institute. Charlie had become a student again with a new process to learn. According to friend and fellow artist Paul Pletka, "Charlie just attacked the medium." He could have failed at this new process. At the very least he might have been intimidated. Charlie, however, thrived on this new experience.

The Culture and the Tradition

Northern New Mexico was an isolated land until the early 1900s. The church had a difficult time becoming established in New Mexico, starting with the Pueblo Revolt of 1680. This caused religion to grow in a unique way in this new land – small village

TOP: San José retablo, 1986. Size: 12" x 16". Watercolor paints. Honorable Mention, 1986 Spanish Market. Private Collection. Photo by artist.

BOTTOM: San José y Guadalupe double retablo, 1985. Size: 6" x 17". Watercolor paints. Artist's Collection. Photo by Robert Reck.

chapels, small home capillas, and frequently the lack of church authority. Dicta from the Papal Seat took a very long time to filter down to the wild lands of Northern New Mexico. Although Pope Benedict established new ideals for representing the Holy Trinity in 1745, for instance, the Byzantine concept of the Trinity as three identical personages lives on even today. The santos and the view of religion are an evolution that are unique to New Mexico. The santos are one of the few truly indigenous arts in America, paralleling the arts of the Native Americans. Much of the interest in santos today comes directly from the cultural isolation found in New Mexico. Hispanics and Native Americans still follow the tenets of their culture and tradition untainted by the plastic world found in many other places in our country.

Charlie's research into the Spanish Colonial santeros takes him regularly to any available collection, private or institutional. He is especially well known by everyone at the Museum of International Folk Art, where he has even been seen instructing curators to stop wearing the "white gloves" when handling santos. The santos were made to be a part of everyday life. More importantly, it has been determined that glove fibers catch the old paint and gesso and contribute to its flaking.

Charlie has often been called upon to evaluate old collections and to appraise them for sale or insurance purposes. He usually jumps at the chance, not because he is well paid for this service, but rather to have the opportunity to study pieces firsthand. When he looks through the drawers and cabinets at the Museum of International Folk Art, Charlie will tell you how each piece by José Rafael Aragón, Fresquís, Molleno, or the Santo Niño Santero influenced his work. These experiences shaped Charlie's use of gesso relief in framing of retablos and in actual specific works that Charlie has done over the years.

The Future

When you talk to anyone who knows Charlie, there is general agreement that he can do wondrous things in the future, as long as he remains healthy. His days of making dozens of retablos are over. Although he insists that he will still do some small pieces that anyone could afford, his interests now are pulled more to creating large, dramatic pieces that tell a story. He is constantly researching new images that haven't been done.

He admits that he has been thinking back to his high school days when he used to paint in oils and acrylics. New experiences are eagerly anticipated. Charlie has been invited to come back to the Tamarind Institute to do a new series of lithographs during the summer of 1994. The collaborative effort on the altar screen at El Rancho de Golondrinas was especially exciting for Charlie. Doing something that has never been done before is what keeps Charlie Carrillo going, especially when it is still in keeping with the roots and traditions of a santero.

But Charlie Carrillo is also a scholar. He is thinking seriously about several book projects. There are a number of exhibits planned for the future that will feature his as well as other santeros' work. Predictions are for an increased national awareness of the New Mexican santero tradition. This will mean more telephone calls from videographers, reporters, writers, collectors, and curators all anxious to know what Charlie knows. Through it all, the religious dimensions of art will remain the most important aspect in Charlie's life.

TOP: San José retablo, 1994. Size: 13" x 16". Authors' Collection. Photo by Ron Behrmann.

BOTTOM: San Huberto retablo, 1990. Size: 7" x 12.5". Collection of Santa Fe artist Robert Stevens. Photo by Robert Reck.

Charlie Carrillo is a product of the unique culture and tradition found in Northern New Mexico. He is a teacher, a student, an artisan, and a very religious man all wrapped into one being. Every major piece that he creates begins with a lengthy research phase that brings with it a part of the story and the history that makes santos so special to so many people in this part of the world. Charlie is truly one of the masters of the santero tradition.

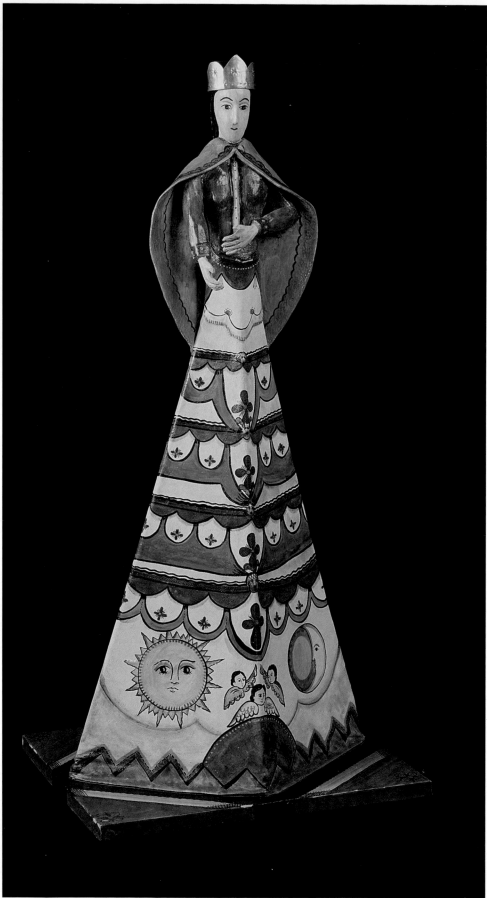

TOP: Charlie exhibiting his work at the 1992 Spanish Market. Photo by Gracie Aldworth.

RIGHT: Nuestra Señora de la Asunción/Our Lady of the Assumption bulto, 1986. Size: 30" tall. Watercolor paints and natural pigments. This is one of Charlie's first hollowframe bultos. Charlie placed a piece of paper inside the frame of this bulto asking whoever finds it to say a prayer to Debbie's grandparents. Private Collection. Photo by Ron Behrmann.

TOP and LEFT: Nuestra Señora del Pueblito de Querétaro/Our Lady of the Village of Querétaro bulto, 1994. Size 64" tall. Contains many different santero art forms – hollowframe bulto, regular bulto, gesso relief, retablo, 14k goldleaf, straw applique, and handcut etched silver. Our Lady floats above the shoulders of San Francisco, who is holding three globes symbolizing the three Franciscan Orders, and supported by the celestial angels. El Niño de Praga is in the clouds to her side. Received the E. Boyd Memorial Award at 1994 Spanish Market for originality and expressive design. This is the largest bulto ever made by Charlie. This work is based on several images modeled after a painting by Peter Paul Rubens titled "Allegory in Honor of the Franciscan Order" found in E. Boyd's _Popular Arts of Spanish New Mexico_, pages 82-85. Authors' Collection. Photo by Ron Behrmann.

TOP: Nuestra Señora del Carmen retablo, 1991. Size: 11.25" x 15.5". Collection of Betty Stewart. Photo by Ebbe Banstorp.

BOTTOM: Santa Barbara retablo, 1985. Enscribed on back "Santa Barbara doncella libranos del rayo y de la centella." Size: 5.5" x 10". Collection of Santa Fe artist Robert Stevens. Photo by Robert Reck.

RIGHT: Nuestra Señora de la Purisima Concepción bulto, 1988. Size: 9" tall. Private Collection. Photo by Ron Behrmann.

The workshop of José Aragón did lots of images of Nuestra Señora de la Purisima Concepción. Some had a halo around the body. Nuestra Señora de Innocencia is also a major image at the Morada in Abiquiú. These served as the inspiration for this piece; see William Wroth's Christian Images in Hispanic New Mexico, page 126, plate 93. On her shoulders is found a reboso, a New Mexican style shawl.

TOP: La Sagrada Familia/The Holy Family or Nacimiento retablo, 1992. Size: 11" x 13.5". Normally the Virgin is seated and José is seen standing. This represents a change in the normal iconography. Collection of Sandra Banstorp. Photo by Ebbe Banstorp.

BOTTOM: Nuestra Señora del Rosario retablo, 1991. Size: 6.75" x 10". Photo by Craig Varjabedian.

LEFT: Nuestra Señora de la Immaculada Concepción bulto, 1990. Size: 10" tall. Artist's Collection. Photo by Rey Móntez.

This is the first bulto that Charlie made with gesso relief hands. Charlie has kept this piece because he and Debbie had fallen in love with it. Charlie made this piece to reflect the simplicity of a home devotional piece. It was inspired by a piece by Molleno; see E. Boyd's _Popular Arts of Spanish New Mexico_, page 355, Figure 22. There is a striking similarity between the mantel on the two pieces.

TOP: San José bulto, 1991. Size: 21" tall. This piece was commisioned without the Christ Child. Note the tools at the base of the bulto and in his hand. Private Collection. Photo by Rudy Miera.

RIGHT: San José con Niño bulto, 1993. Size: 20" tall. Exhibited as a part of Visiting Artists Show at Jonson Gallery, University of New Mexico in 1994. San José is universally esteemed as the patron saint of the family. He usually is depicted holding the Christ Child and the flowering staff. This latter attribute refers to the miraculous blossoming of his staff during the courtship of Mary, which led to his being selected as her successful suitor. This is very similar to a bulto by José Rafael Aragón; see Larry Frank, New Kingdom of the Saints, page 230, plate 213. San José is Charlie's favorite subject. Authors' Collection. Photo by Robert Reck.

TOP: San José retablo, 1994. Size: 16.5" x 22". Collection of Catherine Carrillo. Photo by Ron Behrmann.

LEFT: San José bulto, 1994. Size: 16.5" tall. Private Collection. Photo by Ron Behrmann.

TOP: *Santo Niño de Praga retablo, 1989. Size: 6" x 9". The inspiration for this piece is José Rafael Aragón. See William Wroth's* Christian Images in Hispanic New Mexico, *page 149, Plate 123. The border was painted with Blue Azurite (Zuni Blue), rare pigment (noted in New Mexico as early as 1604). Private Collection. Photo by Craig Varjabedian.*

RIGHT: *Santo Niño de Praga bulto, 1989. Size: 12" tall. The tin crown for this bulto was made by Bonifacio Sandoval. The image of El Niño de Praga represents celebration of the childhood and kingship of Jesus. Collection of Hugh and Dorothea Morris. Photo by Ron Behrmann.*

"New Mexico is a place where stories were told so that when children walk into places like Chimayó and see the altar screen and the santos they are reminded of their past, their present, and their future. They could read the symbolism in the santos."

Charlie Carrillo

TOP: San Miguel Arcángel retablo, 1993. Size: 4.25" x 6". Exhibited as a part of Albuquerque Museum *1994 Miniatures Show*. Authors' Collection. Photo by Ron Behrmann.

LEFT: San Miguel Arcángel bulto, 1987. Size: 8" tall. Charlie designed this bulto so that the devil appears to be coming up out of the base. Private Collection. Photo by Ron Behrmann.

TOP: *Nuestra Señora de la Conquistadora retablo, 1986. Size: 5.75" x 7". Watercolor paints. Private Collection. Photo by artist.*

BOTTOM: *San Vicente retablo, 1988. Size: 12" x 24". Collection of Santa Fe artist Robert Stevens. Photo by Robert Reck.*

RIGHT: *San Rafael bulto, 1989. Size: 16" tall. Rafael is holding a native rainbow trout. Collection of Sandra Banstorp. Photo by Ebbe Banstorp.*

SAN RAFAEL

TOP: Nuestra Señora de la Purísima Concepción/Our Lady of the Immaculate Conception retablo, 1986. Size: 5.75" x 7". Watercolor paints. Private Collection. Photo by artist.

BOTTOM: San Francisco retablo, 1986. Size: 11" x 14". Watercolor paints and natural pigments. Retablo is made from a floor board from Charlie's grandmother's home. Private Collection. Photo by Ron Behrmann.

LEFT: San Rafael bulto, 1988. Size: 11" tall. San Rafael is holding a native rainbow trout. Private Collection. Photo by Ron Behrmann.

"Santos are objects of art, but they are also objects of devotion. They are in the stories of all of us."

Charlie Carrillo

TOP: San Andres retablo, 1991. Size: 7" x 11". Collection of Ron and Trish Behrmann. Photo by Ron Behrmann.

RIGHT: Adán y Eva/Adam and Eve gesso relief retablo, 1994. Size: 20" x 39". Private Collection. Photo by Ron Behrmann.

THE SANTOS

The Cycle of Religious Dramas and Plays and How They Relate Specifically to Santos

The Christmas Story has been transcribed from a talk Charlie gave in December 1993 at the Palace of the Governors Library. Rather than trying to "re-tell" the story, we decided it had the flavor we wanted in Charlie's own words.

Most times when newcomers come to New Mexico or when they experience New Mexico for only one or two times, they have an uneasiness with our santos because of the way we live with our santos, or the way the santos live with us. Our tradition is that santos are a part of our lives, not just something we hang on our wall, not just something we look to maybe every third day. But rather we talk to our santos. They are part of our lives. We don't just live with our santos. They live with us. We invite them into our homes to live with us.

Most times when we think of santos, we think of what people call the Penitente santos, the very bloody Christ, the Christ they call the scourging, the Lenten type of santos, the santos normally associated with New Mexico and Lent.

ABOVE: Adán y Eva/Adam and Eve 7-color lithograph produced at Tamarind Institute, 1990. Mark Attwood, collaborating printer. Size: 18" x 15". Charlie admits to being fascinated by the story of Adam and Eve. He sees this story as the story of all mankind; it is the story of who we are. The entire picture is based on a series of threes — both vertically and horizontally. In Charlie's version of the story, Eve is pregnant with humanity. The center tableau has the roots of the Tree of Life enveloping the Christ Child with the Virgin Mary and Joseph. Photo by Tamarind Institute.

TOP: Adán y Eva/Adam and Eve retablo, 1991. Size: 7" x 9". This is a very allegorical version of Adam and Eve and the story of the Tree of Life. The cross with its grape vines, wheat, and the skull of Adam are symbols of the Tree of Life and the Eucharist. Charlie borrowed this from several ideas in <u>Mexico: Splendor of Thirty Centuries</u> (esp. page 337) — he wanted to try to present the same message but in a different manner. The bones and border are unusual. Collection of Paul and Nancy Pletka. Photo by Ron Behrmann.

BOTTOM: Adán y Eva/Adam and Eve retablo, 1991. Size: 11" x 16". Authors' Collection. Photo by Ron Behrmann.

The Christmas Story

Very few times do we get to talk about santos and the Christmas traditions. And the reason for that is that most scholars do not promote the idea of Christmas santos.

We look at the many collections and we rarely see any representations of the manger scene, or the naciemientos. And the reason we know that these existed is that people have always told stories. Many of our ancestors could not read or write. But they were very wise. You didn't need to know how to read or write to tell biblical stories. Those who knew how to read or write shared their knowledge with other people. Many times those who could read or write were able to read the stories or perform or tell some of the religious folk dramas of New Mexico.

In colonial New Mexico, the stories told around Christmas time were about the creation. The creation story taught the catechism. The Franciscans that came to New Mexico were involved in teaching non-Catholics — the Pueblo people — the traditions of Catholicism and introducing that in New Mexico.

In New Mexico, we start the Christmas season with Adam and Eve. Adam and Eve, under the tree of knowledge, were the center of a religious drama that was told and acted out starting about December 12.

One of the opening verses of the Adam and Eve story depicts them sitting on a bed of boughs underneath the Tree of Knowledge:

<u>In Spanish</u>

Guerra és lá vída del hómbre

En la estación de sú império,

Dé morir en la campaña, irrevocable el decreto.

<u>In English</u>

"War is the life of man in the station of his empire; the irrevocable decree gives death in this campaign."

That story introduced Hispanic and New Mexican children alike to the story of creation and Christmas. The story is that Lucifer summoned all the powers to be to help dethrone man. Lucifer understood that man has been given a special place in the creation. Lucifer decided to send appetite (hunger) in the form of himself or a serpent to tempt Eve to pick the forbidden fruit from the tree. At that point Adam and Eve realize for the first time that they are naked. Saint Michael then shows Adam and Eve the way out of the garden.

(Artist's Note: There are no fig trees in New Mexico, but for obvious reasons you rarely see Adam and Eve covering themselves with pine boughs.)

Then the story continues that Mercy intercedes and asks God to allow Adam and Eve some way out of this situation that caused the great original sin. So Mercy convinces Lucifer to allow redemption.

Redemption is when Christmas actually starts. You have Saint Michael the Archangel throwing Adam and Eve out. In New Mexico, Lucifer is usually depicted as a rattlesnake. Native Americans opposed this depiction because snakes are a sacred animal in Puebloan mythology. Saint Michael is sometimes seen with some conflict in the two cultures.

Because He used Saint Michael to evict Adam and Eve and because He also promised redemption, God had to send a second archangel, Gabriel, to announce to Mary that she would become pregnant with Christ and that Christ would be brought to the world as the redeemer. Hence the story of Gabriel of the Annunciation, another retablo (image) used for storytelling in New Mexico.

You can't have a birth of course without a pregnant virgin. Our Lady of Guadalupe is the Hispanic story of that pregnant virgin. It is a simple story of the Virgin who looked like a Native American. The story was set in the period of Juan Diego. Juan Diego was not a lowly, poor native as has been depicted in many versions. He was a bright, intelligent young man of noble Indian descent in the early 1500s in Mexico. The church wanted the people to believe that he was a common man. But the truth of the matter is very different.

The story is that the virgin appeared to Juan Diego, a Náhuatl Indian in Tepeyac in Mexico. She appeared as a pregnant virgin — symbolized by the tassels hanging from her waist — to Juan Diego. She talked to him in his native Aztec language. He asked her what he should call her and she said Qualachupe. In Náhuatl, the Aztec language, Qualachupe

TOP: Adán y Eva/Adam and Eve retablo, 1994. Size: 14" x 19". Collection of J. Cacciola Gallery, New York, NY. Photo by Ron Behrmann.

BOTTOM: Adán y Eva/Adam and Eve retablo, 1991. Size: 17.25" x 31". Exhibited as a part of the ¡Chispas! show at the Heard Museum. Collection of Mr. and Mrs. Charlie Sánchez. Photo by Ron Behrmann.

LEFT: San Miguel Arcángel retablo, 1988. Size: 11" x 15". Artist's Collection. Photo by Robert Reck.

translates as "the woman who crushes the head of the serpent." This is the way Catholic dogma was introduced to the new lands. Qualachupe became Guadalupe.

She asked him to tell the bishop to build a shrine in her honor. Of course, the bishop needed further convincing and asked for a sign. When Juan Diego returned to the original site, the vision of Mary reappeared. She told Juan Diego to take back to the bishop fresh roses that miraculously appeared all around her on the hillside; it was the middle of winter. The vision arranged the roses in Juan Diego's cloak. When the cloak was presented to the bishop, the roses fell to the floor and the image of Mary appeared on the cloth. The image of Our Lady of Guadalupe is usually pictured wearing a turquoise mantle with stars symbolizing the mestizo race.

The feast day of Guadalupe is December 12 and this begins the Christmas Season. The feast day for San Nicholas was the week before on December 6. Our Lady of Guadalupe has been the patroness of the Americas and especially Native Americans and Hispanic peoples since 1531.

We start with San Nicholas and then come to the Virgin. We introduce the concept of the pregnant woman bringing the redemption to New Mexico and the whole New World order. Beyond the introduction of Our Lady of Guadalupe, Santa María, Saint Michael, the Christ Child, and Adam and Eve, the most important thing is the cycle of religious dramas.

There were four dramas played out in New Mexico: the creation and the expulsion of Adam and Eve is the first in the cycle, and the crucifixion (the ultimate story) ends the cycle.

Coloquio de San José

The Coloquio de San José is the story of how San José or Saint Joseph was picked as the spouse of the Virgin Mary. San José is always pictured with his staff. The story starts with Simeon handing out a decree to all potential patriarchs — "the ruling father" — in his territory summoning them to the temple. Each of the men was to bring a staff to the temple. Joseph was one of the available bachelors. The story was that there was a virgin who was to be married off and seven eligible men showed up at the temple. The men were called by a herald named Feliciano who reminded them that they each must bring a staff. When Joseph showed up with the other bachelors who were available as spouses of the Virgin, his staff miraculously bloomed into flower — a symbol from God that Joseph was the chosen one. In Native American as well as Hispanic cultures, the flower is seen as a fertility symbol. New Mexicans never forgot that story; they always included a flowering staff when they depicted San José in retablos or bultos. San José is also sometimes seen with a hat and a basket with his carpentry tools. The flowering staff has become a standard in New Mexican iconography among the santeros. In New Mexico, the flowering staff is called the "vara de San José" which in English translates to hollyhocks. As a young boy I remember hearing people talking about the beautiful hollyhocks and how pretty the pink ones were. Growing up I thought that they were talking about some strange pink bird — a holy hawk. I didn't make the connection with vara de San José. In New Mexico, even botanical names revolved around the catechism.

Las Posadas y Los Pastores

In New Mexican Hispanic villages, beginning nine nights before Christmas, individuals dressed as Joseph and the Virgin Mary would set out to ask for lodging from various houses. Each night they would be turned away until the last night on which they

TOP: San Miguel Arcángel retablo, 1991. Size: 5.5" x 9". Collection of Mark and Joanna Metzbower. Photo by Ron Behrmann.

BOTTOM: San Miguel Arcángel/ Saint Michael the Archangel retablo, 1987. Size: 5.5" x 8". Artist's Collection. Photo by Robert Reck.

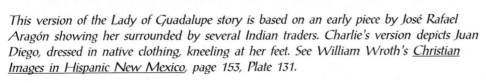

TOP: *Nuestra Señora de Guadalupe bulto, 1991. Size: 7" tall. Authors' Collection. Photo by Craig Varjabedian.*

BOTTOM: *Nuestra Señora de Guadalupe retablo, 1989. Size: 11.75" x 16". Private Collection. Photo by Craig Varjabedian.*

LEFT: *Nuestra Señora de Guadalupe retablo, 1990. Size: 11.5" x 17.5". Collection of Barbara and Bill Douglas. Photo by Robert Reck.*

This version of the Lady of Guadalupe story is based on an early piece by José Rafael Aragón showing her surrounded by several Indian traders. Charlie's version depicts Juan Diego, dressed in native clothing, kneeling at her feet. See William Wroth's <u>Christian Images in Hispanic New Mexico</u>, page 153, Plate 131.

TOP: Nuestra Señora de Guadalupe en nicho, 1990. Size: Bulto 16" tall; nicho 23" tall. Private Collection. Photo by Craig Varjabedian.

RIGHT: Nuestra Señora de Guadalupe bulto, 1989. Size: 16" tall. Private Collection. Photo by Craig Varjabedian.

are finally given a place to stay, in the manger. In this drama the couple would sing a verse asking for lodging.

This is the second story in the teachings or dramas about Christmas; it is called "Las Posadas" – the story of Joseph and the Virgin Mary ready to give birth seeking lodging. Nowadays, at the end of each night, the couple is let in, symbolic of human goodness. It is celebrated with hot chocolate, coffee, and biscochitos.

In many of the Posadas stories, the devil is actually a part of the drama. The devil is a symbol of temptation or of human conscience. The story goes that the houses of Christians had a cross at the doorway. Christians would dare pass the threshold past the cross, but the devil can't pass by. Instead he would go from door to door soliciting help from the person at the door dressed as a handsome debonair gentleman. When they did come out, the devil could enter. Any young girl who smiled at a stranger in the house could find herself on the devil's list. The part of the devil in the Christmas story was to remind us that evil is always around us and if we are not careful, evil can screw us up – as well as a lesson not to be too friendly with strangers. Actually this is a double play or story which includes "Las Posadas" followed by "Los Pastores" or "La Pastorela," the drama of the shepherds bringing gifts to Bethlehem for the Christ Child and the struggle of good over evil. This drama with its many characters, especially Bartolo the lazy shepherd, was often very long, but it served as a morality play which taught Catholic morality and instructed the young and old alike in the Christmas mystery.

"Los Pastores" is followed by "Los Tres Reyes Magos" – the Three Wise Men or Kings. Kings' day is celebrated in New Mexico on January 6.

Los Tres Reyes Magos

New Mexico used to celebrate the three kings drama, but the script for this drama has been lost. The story was that the three kings visited Herod, staying at his palace on the way to the star in the East. The three wise men on their return from visiting Bethlehem decided not to divulge the location of the Christ Child. The Tres Reyes story ends with San José as the central figure again, when he has a dream. An angel appears in San José's dream saying that he is in trouble; he can't go back because Herod is killing the innocents, the massacre of the innocents. The angel told Joseph to flee into Egypt, to take flight – La Huida a Egipto, which is the story told on many early retablos as a teaching device to instruct children about the story of Christmas.

One of the parts of the Tres Reyes story that has been lost is the story of El Niño Perdido, or the Lost Christ Child. The New Mexican story is about the defiant Christ Child who ran away from home and ended up in the palace of a very wealthy king. The Christ Child attended a banquet with all kinds of fabulous foods served by the king who was really a messenger from Lucifer. Lucifer tempted the Christ Child by asking several important questions for which the Christ Child had great answers for each. Lucifer was so overwhelmed by the Christ Child's responses that he sent the Christ Child out. The Christ Child ended up at the temple where he spellbound the doctors of the temple. Several days later his parents found him and scolded him. His parents told him that he defied his parents and that he had been a bad child. His response to his parents was that he was only doing his Father's work. This is again a teaching tool for the Christmas story. Many New Mexican retablos depict San José, the Virgin mother and the Christ Child reunited – La Sagrada Familia – a very common image in colonial stories, while other images depict the Niño Perdido, or the lost child.

TOP: La Huida a Egipto/Flight from Egipto retablo, 1993. Size: 8" x 13". Authors' Collection. Photo by Ron Behrmann.

BOTTOM: La Huida a Egipto/ Flight from Egypt retablo, 1986. Size: 7.75" x 14". Private Collection. Photo by Craig Varjabedian.

San Antonio

The final story in the Christmas cycle has to do with San Antonio. Many people, especially in New Mexico, look to San Antonio when they have lost something. San Antonio is the saint that everyone turned to — New Mexican grandmothers, *tíos y tías*, moms and dads — when something couldn't be found. He was stuck in the corner, punished, and reminded as a real person he was to keep watch out for the lost item. He was also the one who was frequently punished when those items couldn't be found.

TOP: La Huida a Egipto/Flight from Egypt retablo, 1990. Size: 7.75" x 16". Private Collection. Photo by Craig Varjabedian.

BOTTOM: San Antonio oval retablo, 1989. Size: 6.5" x 11". Collection of Jennifer Martinez and William McArthur. Photo by Robert Reck.

RIGHT: San Antonio de Padua bulto, 1993. Size: 12" tall. Collection of Ebbe Banstorp. Photo by Craig Varjabedian.

Every Hispanic family has a story about San Antonio and something that was lost and how he helped them find it. Curiously, he was also the one who found available worthy young husbands for unmarried girls. This was not the story of young vain women seeking husbands, but rather an important part of catechism. If you are going to ask a saint for help, it should be for something worthy. After asking San Antonio to help find a worthy husband, many would pray to San Antonio to allow them to become pregnant. San Antonio was probably at many a conception in New Mexico! This may sound sacrilegious, but saints have always been seen in New Mexico as an integral part of people's lives.

My family has a wonderful story involving San Antonio. It was only recently that I confirmed the story with my *Tia*. Sometime in my early childhood, perhaps one of the times my family was at my Nana's house in Belen, I heard the story from her. In New Mexico colloquial Spanish, when the word "Nana" is used, it is like saying "Grandma."

It was during the early spring time that the story of San Antonio begins to take place, although he isn't in the picture until late spring. Apparently my Grandmother Ignacia Abeyta Carrillo had planted her garden and had already spent considerable effort in transplanting chili seedlings and thinning other vegetable plants when a tremendous hail storm destroyed the home garden. My grandmother had been widowed twice and the family of five children needed the garden to make it through the year. Heartbroken, she replanted her garden, and in so doing lost her wedding ring in the garden soil. Having great faith in San Antonio, Nana went back to her house where she took the plaster of Paris statue of San Antonio from his place on her dresser and carried him to a massive cottonwood tree near the garden. This plaster statue was not a traditional New Mexican santo carved from wood, those were already long gone from the village of Abeytas. However this image was her favorite and she sternly reminded him that he was about to be put into a hollow of this massive cottonwood tree, from which he had the vantage point of her entire garden. He was instructed to do two things: first, he was to make sure that no more hail storms or natural disasters were to damage the garden, and second, since he was always looking at the garden, day and night, he was to keep his eyes open for her lost wedding band.

The day finally arrived that my grandmother was finished with her harvest, and in thanksgiving she hurried to the hollow in the tree where she had placed San Antonio many months before. She decided that since the garden had been extra productive despite the early setback, she was going to thank San Antonio. As she reached in the hollow of the tree, she sadly realized that something was terribly wrong. It seems that the late summer rains had caused the hollow in the tree to drip water, and the slow but steady drip had eaten away most of the head of her beloved santo. With tears in her eyes, she reached in for her San Antonio, lifted him and, to her amazement, her lost wedding ring was resting underneath the base of her Antonio. Truly he was "milagroso;" he had watched over the garden and protected it from harm, and he had even recovered her ring, despite the fact that he had no eyes with which to see.

TOP: San Antonio de Padua bulto, 1989. Photo taken at 1989 Spanish Market by Fred Cisneros.

BOTTOM: San Antonio retablo, 1990. Size: 7" x 10". Charlie's friend Luís Tapia asked him to restore an old retablo by José Rafael Aragón. After Charlie stabilized the piece, he made an exact copy, one of the only copies Charlie has ever made. It reminds him of the effectiveness of a simple design. Artist's Collection. Photo by Robert Reck.

The last time I remember seeing my Grandmother's santo was when she passed away. I was not yet six years old, but I can vividly recall the image placed next to her coffin during the traditional "velatorio" or wake that was held in her home. I wanted to cry the other day when I found out that her San Antonio was still with my Tia in Belen, and despite his adventures in the hollow of the large cottonwood tree in Abeytas, New Mexico, some fifty year ago, he remains true to those who believe in him.

Other stories about San Antonio involve threats to him if he didn't do as he promised. Many San Antonio bultos have a removable Christ Child. In the days of old, San Antonio would be threatened "If you don't shape up, Tony, and find whatever it was that

I lost, I'll take away Baby Jesus from you." That was one of the most severe punishments you could give San Antonio. Many museum collections of older San Antonio bultos are missing the Baby Jesus — it appears that the Baby Jesus was left behind many times. There must be many stories in Hispanic families that have San Antonio as a central character. New Mexican tradition also has San Antonio involved in some way with El Niño Perdido, the Lost Christ Child. New Mexican stories have San Antonio finding the Christ Child.

San Isidro

Another story deals with San Isidro, the patron of farmers. This story could be told in almost any Hispanic village or Pueblo. The story goes that after many years of watching over farming, San Isidro was getting tired. Everyone was saying that he must be tired, he had been working for 200 years. Maybe he ought to get a break. So they gave him a break and brought out the Santo Niño de Atocha. They brought out the Santa Niño because he was a young boy who could work hard. Maybe he would understand what the farmers needed. So the people processed Santo Niño de Atocha through the fields, as they had done with San Isidro praying for rain. San Isidro was so tired maybe the Santo Niño would help bring rain. Unfortunately Santo Niño sent them too much rain, way too much rain. It rained and rained and washed all the fields and crops away. The people

TOP: La Anunciación/The Annunciation retablo, 1988. Size: 12" x 20". The Holy Spirit is seen shining down on Mary as she prays, while Gabriel hands her a bouquet of flowers as he announces that God has chosen her to be the mother of Jesus. For another version of this story see Larry Frank's New Kingdom of the Saints, *page 162, plate 135. Private Collection. Photo by artist.*

BOTTOM: La Anunciación/The Annunciation retablo, 1994. Size: 15" x 19.25". Private Collection. Photo by Ron Behrmann.

ABOVE: La Sagrada Familia bulto, 1990. Size: 23" tall. Collection of Keith and Letta Wofford. Photo by Craig Varjabedian. This was one of Charlie's first bultos of the Holy Family. He carved the three figures first. He made the nicho as a way to create a "home" for the family. The Holy Spirit is found at the top of the nicho, symbolized by the dove.

were devastated. They then said, "Look what Santo Niño has done. San Isidro would never have done this. How could he do this?" They felt so bad that the next morning they took out the Niño's mother, the Virgin Mother. They carried a bulto of Nuestra Señora de los Dolores – Our Lady of Sorrows – to the fields. Tears appeared in her eyes looking at the devastation in the fields that her son had brought on the farmers. They say to her, "Look what your bad little boy has brought on us." This is a typical Hispanic New Mexican reaction. We live with our saints and we are not afraid to criticize even the Christ Child. To Hispanics, this is not sacrelegious. In New Mexican tradition, if a saint

Tamarind Invites: Lithographs by New Mexican Santeros was the first time the University of New Mexico's Tamarind Institute collaborated with santeros to print lithographs. The santeros invited were: Charlie Carrillo, Felix López, Ramón José López, Eluid Martinez, Anita Romero Jones, and Luís Tapia. Following the production of the lithographs an exhibit opened in January, 1991, at the Museum of International Folk Art. A second show was later held at the Harwood Foundation in Taos. According to Helen Lucero, curator at the time of the exhibit at Folk Art, "The project gave the santeros an opportunity to take traditional folk art into a fine art medium." The idea of the santero project came from Bill Lagatutta, master printer at the Tamarind. Senior printers Julie Maher, Cole Rogers and Mark Attwood assisted the santeros.

TOP: La Sagrada Familia retablo, 1980. Size: 12" x 9.25". Acrylic paint on commercial board. Collection of Jimmy and Debbie Trujillo. Photo by Robert Reck.

BOTTOM: San Isidro retablo, 1991. Size: 17" x 23". Private Collection. Photo by Ron Behrmann.

LEFT: San Isidro 7-color lithograph produced at Tamarind Institute 1990. Mark Attwood, collaborating printer. Size: 15" x 18". Photo by Tamarind Institute.

blows it, you punish him. This is at the core of Christianity, where Christ is human. Not just the Godhead of Christ, but also the Manhood of Christ. Being human is being prone to mistakes. This is a beautiful way of teaching the tenets of our faith and religion — catechism incorporating the saints and teaching the humanity of Christ.

TOP: La Visitación/The Visitation retablo, 1994. Size: 17" x 19". Larry Frank's New Kingdom of the Saints, page 166, plate 137 explains the story as the meeting between Zacharias and Elizabeth (the mother of Saint John the Baptist) and Mary and Joseph. Collection of Jennifer Martinez and William McArthur. Photo by Ron Behrmann.

BOTTOM: La Sagrada Familia/The Holy Family retablo, 1988. Size: 12" x 18". Private Collection. Photo by artist.

RIGHT: La Sagrada Familia/The Holy Family retablo, 1989. Size: 12" x 18". Private Collection. Photo by Craig Varjabedian.

Charlie designed this retablo to represent the earthly trinity — Joseph, Mary, and Jesus — as well as the Holy/Celestial Trinity in the vertical dimension. God the Father is seen at the top, with the Holy Spirit (the dove) in the center. The lamb (Christ) is at the bottom. This is the first time that Charlie depicted the Virgin seated in a chair. The inspiration for the arch and the columns came from the wall painting that Charlie did at the Museum of International Folk Art (see page 52).

TOP: San José con Niño retablo, 1990. Size: 7.25" x 13". Collection of Bill and Barbara Douglas. Photo by Robert Reck.

BOTTOM: San José con Niño retablo, 1991. Size: 11.75" x 17". See Robin Farwell Gavins' *Traditional Arts of Spanish New Mexico*, page 42. Private Collection. Photo by Craig Varjabedian.

LEFT: San José con Niño bulto, 1987. Size: 20" tall. Private Collection. Photo by Kirk Gittings.

ABOVE: San José Patriarca bulto, 1994. Size: 24" tall. Gift to the Santa María de la Paz Catholic Community, Santa Fe. Photo by Ron Behrmann.

Charlie offered to donate a San José to the Santa María de la Paz Catholic Community as it was first being planned. The arts committee asked him to do the San José for the Marian Chapel. The nicho was unusually wide and Charlie remembered a San José in Roland Dickey's New Mexico Village Arts where San José stood with the baby next to him with their hands outstretched to each other. Charlie wanted San José's hand to guard the Christ Child in a more fatherly way. It has been pointed out that the throne resembles something found in the Jewish temple — the chair of Elijah which was used for ceremonial purposes. Symbolic blood is dripping down the sides of the throne, a reference to the first bloodshed of Christ, his circumcision. The tree in the foreground comes from Renaissance paintings and symbolizes new life as well as the object of the carpenter's craft. The dominant colors on San José are green, red and yellow, symbolizing new life, marriage, and fertility. Charlie wanted this piece to be a teaching tool to all who view it.

TOP: *Santa Barbara retablo, 1991. Size: 7.75" x 13". Private Collection. Photo by Craig Varjabedian.*

LEFT: *Nuestra Señora de la Imaculada Concepción/Our Lady of the Immaculate Conception retablo with gesso relief, 1993. Size: 14.5" x 48". First Prize retablo winner at 1993 Spanish Market. Exhibited as a part of the Albuquerque Museum Charles M. Carrillo: Santos show in 1993 to celebrate "The Year of American Craft: A Celebration of the Creative Work of the Hand." Charlie had a concept for making this piece for several years, but he never seemed to have the right piece of wood. One day as he was shaping a piece of pine, he realized that he had the right piece for this retablo. Charlie indicates that this piece was influenced by both the Laguna Santero and by Bernardo Miera y Pacheco. See E. Boyd's Popular Arts of Spanish New Mexico, page 107, Figure 89. Charlie says that of all the gesso relief pieces that he has done, he is most satisfied with this one. Authors' Collection. Photo by Ron Behrmann.*

TOP: *Nuestra Señora del Camino retablo, 1989. Size: 6.5 x 11.5". A source for this subject can be found in Mitchell Wilder and Edgar Breitenbach's Santos, The Religious Folk Art of New Mexico, Plate 55. Private Collection. Photo by owner.*

BOTTOM: *La Huida a Egipto/ Flight to Egypt retablo, 1988. Size: 18" x 24". Albuquerque International Airport Collection. Photo by Damian Andrus.*

RIGHT: *La Sagrada Familia/ The Holy Family retablo, 1991. Latin inscription Parvulus Natus Est Nobis (Unto Us Is Born A Child). Size: 10" x 22". Private Collection. Photo by Craig Varjabedian.*

Icons used by santeros

An ancient symbol of God the Father is the heart. It was frequently used in pictures of the Trinity. The symbol of the Holy Spirit is the dove, and a baby is the symbol of Christ. Joseph is frequently dressed not in ancient clothes but rather as a man dressed in more contemporary clothing – in the 1700s or 1800s in colonial dress. This was a way for New Mexicans to place Joseph not in the historic past but rather in the present, in clothing of the day, making him one of them. It is not uncommon to see the Virgin on a burro with Joseph wearing a Rio Grande blanket over his shoulder or with a brand on the hindquarters of the burro. The use of the brand has even helped modern santeros to identify our older santeros. Threes, fives, sevens, and nines are sacred symbols for santeros in New Mexico.

LEFT: Nuestra Señora de la Imaculada Concepción/Our Lady of the Immaculate Conception bulto, 1992. Size: 28.5" tall. Private Collection. Photo by Ron Behrmann.

TOP: Santo Niño de Atocha retablo, 1988. Size: 7.75" x 13". The model for this piece is a retablo by José Rafael Aragón. See E. Boyd's *Popular Arts of Spanish New Mexico*, page 391, plate 32. Private Collection. Photo by Craig Varjabedian.

BOTTOM: San Antonio hide painting, 1988. Size: 18" x 36". Private Collection. Photo by Ron Behrmann.

RIGHT: Familia y Fe/Family and Faith painting, 1987. Size: 120" x 144". Found at the entrance of Museum of International Folk Art Hispanic Heritage Wing. Photo by William Goldman.

After the Museum of International Folk Art asked him to paint this piece, William Wroth came to Charlie with a retablo by José Rafael Aragón to use as a prototype. Several watercolor renditions preceeded the actual wall painting. The unique staff in Joséph's hand is a flowering corn stalk, a tribute to Native American traditions. The elements at the top of the wall painting are similar to those by José Aragón in a reredos; see Marta Weigle's *Hispanic Arts and Ethnohistory*, page 218, figure 1, William Wroth's *Christian Images in Hispanic New Mexico*, page 142, plate 114 and Robin Farwell Gavins' *Traditional Arts of Spanish New Mexico*, page 59.

BOTTOM: Santiago Pelegrino retablo, 1994. Size: 6" x 13.5". Authors' Collection. Photo by Ron Behrmann.

LEFT: San Isidro Labrador/Saint Isidore the Farmer retablo, 1989. Size: 20" x 46.5". Charlie had been saving this piece of wood for a while, waiting to do a big piece that told a story that had a lot of symbolism. The staff is called a dejarratadera or a hocking staff, used to stun the tendons of animals, such as oxen, and thus keep them in line and from running away. It was also a medieval torture tool. The angel spreading the seeds is rare, as are the two angels at the bottom – three total angels are also part of the iconography. The cutouts on the edge are taken from Spanish Colonial/ New Mexican furniture designs, especially benches. The dove at the top symbolizes the Holy Spirit and is inside a large stylized sunflower. There are five flowers on each side symbolizing the five wounds of Christ. Collection of Paul and Nancy Pletka. Photo by Ron Behrmann.

TOP: San Isidro retablo, 1988. Size: 18" x 24". Collection of Keith and Letta Wofford. Photo by Robert Reck.

BOTTOM: San Isidro retablo, 1991. Size: 7.75" x 11". Private Collection. Photo by Craig Varjabedian.

RIGHT: San Isidro gesso relief retablo, 1994. Size: 20" x 49.5". Cantilevered cross with handcut etched silver. Received the Florence Dibell Bartlett Award at 1994 Spanish Market for innovative design. The inspiration for this piece came to Charlie in a dream two weeks before Spanish Market. This retablo took over 60 hours of work to complete. Collection of JoAnn and Robert Balzer. Photo by Ron Behrmann.

TOP: San Isidro retablo, 1991. Size: 8" x 16.5". Collection of Ron and Trish Behrmann. Photo by Ron Behrmann.

LEFT: San Isidro Labrador gesso relief retablo, 1993. Size: 16" x 33.75". Hand-adzed ponderosa pine, homemade gesso, natural pigments, piñon sap varnish. Exhibited as a part of the Albuquerque Museum Charles M. Carrillo: Santos show in 1993 to celebrate "The Year of American Craft: A Celebration of the Creative Work of the Hand." Collection of The Albuquerque Museum, purchased from 1991 General Obligation Bonds (93.048.001). Photo by Robert Reck.

TOP LEFT: San Isidro retablo, 1993. Size: 13.75" x 19.75". Collection of and photo by The Denver Art Museum.

TOP RIGHT: San Isidro Labrador bulto, 1990 along with five other retablos. San Isidro bulto was the 1990 Spanish Market Grand Prize winner. Size: bulto 13" tall; base 22" x 7" tall. Exhibited as a part of the Crafting Devotion: Tradition in Contemporary New Mexican Santos show at the Gene Autry Museum. One model for this piece was José Benito Ortega. See Thomas Steele's Santos and Saints, page 144, E. Boyd's Popular Arts of Spanish New Mexico, page 417, plate 211 and Robin Farwell Gavins' Traditional Arts of Spanish New Mexico, page 65. Collection of Gene Autry Museum, Los Angeles. Photo by Craig Varjabedian.

BOTTOM RIGHT: Reredos/Altar screen with Nuestra Señora del Carmen, San Isidro, San José and God the Father at the top, 1983. Size: 48" x 24". Acrylic paints. Collection of Barbara and Bill Douglas. Photo by Robert Reck.

Charlie feels that the story that many people have about the Santo Niño de Atocha is incorrect. The Santo Niño de Atocha is a Mexican devotional image, whereas his mother is a Spanish image. Charlie notes that Yvonne Lange correctly wrote in El Palacio Magazine in 1978 about the Santo Niño being a Mexican devotion. All the images above are based on a late 19th Century chromolithic style similar to Currier & Ives and others rather than the Mexican style of the Santo Niño de Atocha. The New Mexican style is always simpler and the dress is less elaborate (eg., a feather in the hat rather than an ostrich plume). Charlie grew up with the chromolithic style images. As a santero, he has explored the New Mexican style.

TOP: Santo Niño de Atocha bulto, 1991. Size: 9" tall. Private Collection. Photo by Craig Varjabedian.

BOTTOM: Santo Niño de Atocha retablo, 1987. Size: 5.75" x 9". See Thomas Steele's Santos and Saints, page 112; notice the striking similarity to the retablo by José Rafael Aragón. Private Collection. Photo by Craig Varjabedian.

LEFT: Four Santo Niño de Atocha retablos. Clockwise from upper left: 9" x 12" on canvas, 1980; 9" x 12", 1981; 11" x 17", 1983; and 9" x 13" on tin, 1984. All four retablos were made with acrylic paints. Artist's Collection. Photos by Robert Reck.

TOP: San Cristobal retablo, 1994. Size: 5.5" x 8". See E. Boyd's *Popular Arts of Spanish New Mexico*, page 439, figure 221. Authors' Collection. Photo by Ron Behrmann.

RIGHT: Santo Niño de Atocha bulto, 1989. Size: 8" tall. Cottonwood root, natural pigments, homemade gesso, and elkskin leather hat. Private Collection. Photo by Kirk Gittings.

Charlie did this piece so that he could have a small devotional piece of the Santo Niño in a New Mexican setting. The chair was carved as a colonial New Mexican chair – it is made up of some 20 pieces. The chair took as long to make as the bulto itself. The two flowers or bushes in the foreground are reminiscent of José Rafael Aragón. This piece was included in Elmo Baca and Suzanne Deats' book *Santa Fe Design*, 1990, page 232.

TOP: Santo Niño de Atocha retablo in contemporary clothing, 1991. Size: 11.25" x 15". Collection of William Hart McNichols. Photo by Mary Elkins.

LEFT: Santo Niño de Atocha retablo in contemporary clothing, 1993. Size: 14" x 24". Most Santo Niño de Atochas were done in colonial dress, which was contemporary dress for the santeros that made them. After much research, Charlie realized that this image should be done in the dress of the times as his ancestors would have done. Exhibited as a part of the Albuquerque Museum *Charles M. Carrillo: Santos* show in 1993 to celebrate "The Year of American Craft: A Celebration of the Creative Work of the Hand" and at the *Visiting Artists Show* at Jonson Gallery, University of New Mexico in 1994. Authors' Collection. Photo by Ron Behrmann.

TOP: La Alma de la Virgen retablo, 1993. Size: 6" x 9.5". Charlie's inspiration for this came from a piece by José Rafael Aragón at the Harwood Foundation in Taos. He was taken by the hands that looked like a dove. Collection of Jennifer Martinez and William McArthur. Photo by Robert Reck.

BOTTOM: Nuestra Señora de la Luz/Our Lady of Light retablo, 1989. Size: 12" x 15". Collection of Sandra Banstorp. Photo by Ebbe Banstorp.

RIGHT: Nuestra Señora de la Imaculada Concepción bulto, 1989. Size: 9.5" tall. Collection of Barbara and Bill Douglas. Photo by Robert Reck.

TOP: *Nuestra Señora de Loretto retablo*, 1994. Size: 10.25" x 15". Private Collection. Photo by Ron Behrmann.

LEFT: *Nuestra Señora de la O/de la Esperanza with Christ Child in reliquary, hollowframe bulto*, 1993. Size: 48" tall. Exhibited as a part of the Albuquerque Museum <u>Charles M. Carrillo: Santos</u> show in 1993 to celebrate "The Year of American Craft: A Celebration of the Creative Work of the Hand." About eight years before he did this piece, Charlie had seen several medieval paintings of Our Lady. These paintings showed the Virgin with her body as a tabernacle. Charlie kept these images in his mind until he was ready to make her into a bulto. The Christ Child in the reliquary has wounds as an allegory. As a symbol of salvation, the Virgin is seen as a tabernacle for the Christ Child. There is a saying in the Penitente Brotherhood that relates directly to this piece: <u>"Y pues tú, por espacio de nueve meses, tuvites mis entráñas por morada."</u> ("And for you, for a period of nine months, you occupied my body as your dwelling place.") Private Collection. Photo by Robert Reck.

TOP: Charlie Carrillo holding the first prize retablo at the 1993 Spanish Market. Photo by Barbe Awalt.

RIGHT: Santo Niño de Nacimiento bulto, 1993. Hand-carved Niño with detachable halo & inset of mica, lace robe from the Abiquiú Morada. Latin inscription: Parvulus Natus Est Nobis/Unto Us Is Born A Child. Size: 4" x 12.5". Exhibited as a part of Visiting Artists Show at Jonson Gallery, University of New Mexico in 1994. Many santeros did the Christ Child in a manger, including José Rafael Aragón. See Larry Franks' New Kingdom of the Saints, page 233, plate 216. Authors' Collection. Photo by Ron Behrmann.

TOP: Nuestra Señora del Rosario/ Our Lady of the Rosary retablo, 1994. Size: 13.5" x 17". Collection of Ana Montoya. Photo by Ron Behrmann.

BOTTOM: Nuestra Señora de San Juan de los Lagos/Our Lady of St. John of the Lakes retablo, 1986. Size: 4.75" x 8". Watercolor paints. Private Collection. Photo by artist.

LEFT: El Niño Jesús bulto with mica and tin halo, 1992. Size: 9.5" tall. Christ Child has allegorical wounds on the hands and feet. Collection of Mr. and Mrs. Samuel Larcombe. Photo by Robert Reck.

TOP: La Divina Pastora/The Divine Shepherdess retablo, 1986. Size: 4.75" x 8". Watercolor paints. Inspired by José Aragón; see Marta Weigle's *Hispanic Arts and Ethnohistory*, page 261, figure 26. Private Collection. Photo by artist.

RIGHT: La Divina Pastora/The Divine Shepherdess bulto, 1994. Size: 10" tall. Authors' Collection. Photo by Robert Reck.

In 1987, one of Charlie's friends brought him an old bulto to identify. It was of a woman sitting in a chair. She had no other identifying marks and Charlie couldn't be sure who it was. After some preliminary research, he thought it must be Saint Ann, Saint Agnes, or La Divina Pastora. After additional research, he concluded it must be La Divina Pastora. As he was getting ready for Spanish Market in 1993, he was going through Marta Weigle's *Hispanic Arts and Ethnohistory* and came across Divina again. At that time he decided that he wanted to do that piece. After Winter Market, he decided that he needed a small but intricate piece to get back into the feel of carving. Charlie has always said that the smaller they are the harder they are to make. Charlie found that making this piece was a lot of fun to do because he had never done animals before. When he first finished her, her dress came all the way down to the base. He did some more research and found that she usually had shoes. So he redid the bottom of her dress and carved her shoes. Her hat is based on a South American design – the La Divina story came from Spain to Ecuador. The plants or trees are based on a design by José Aragón.

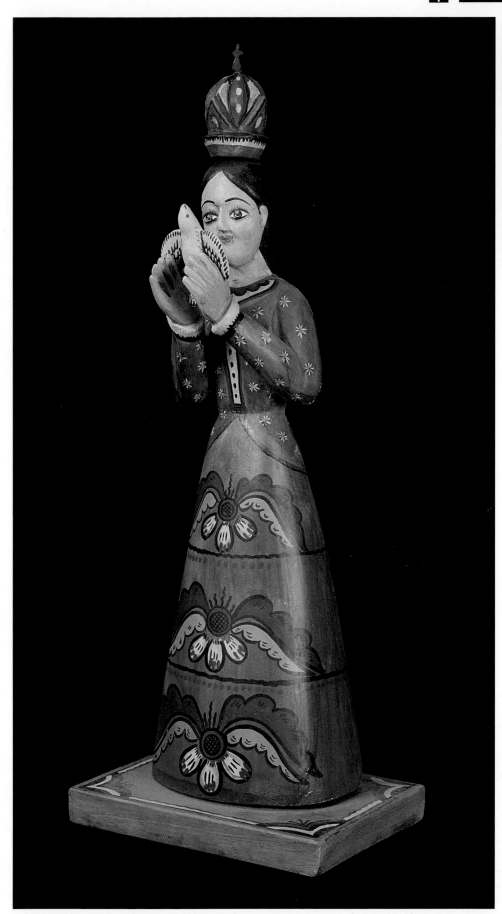

TOP: Nuestra Señora de la Paz/Our Lady of Peace retablo, 1994. Size: 7.5" x 10". Collection of Ron and Trish Behrmann. Photo by Ron Behrmann.

LEFT: Nuestra Señora de la Paz bulto, 1991. Size: 16" tall. Charlie did this piece during the 1991 Gulf War. He wanted to do a Virgin as well as deal with the anxiety and stress of the war. This piece was completed during Lent when Charlie prayed for all involved in the war. It symbolizes both healing and peace. Authors' Collection. Photo by Ron Behrmann.

†

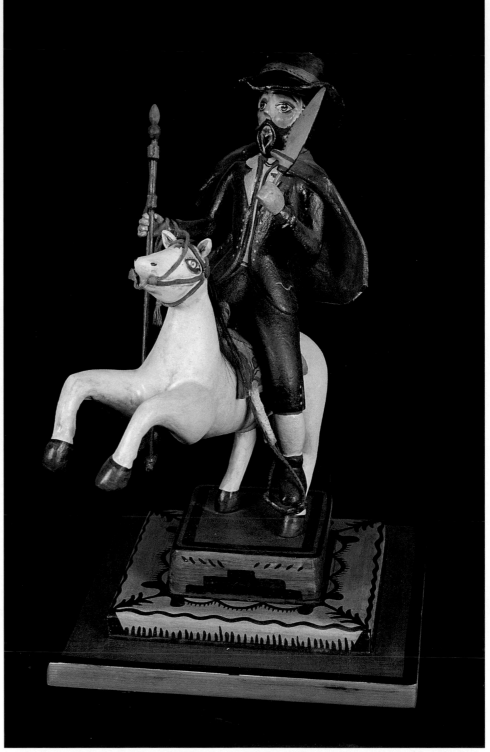

TOP: Santiago retablo, 1991. Size: 11.5" x 16". Collection of Sandra Banstorp. Photo by Ebbe Banstorp.

BOTTOM: Santiago retablo, 1988. Size: 11.5" x 16". Collection of Jennifer Martinez and William McArthur. Photo by Robert Reck.

RIGHT: Santiago/Saint James bulto, 1990. Size: 17" tall. Collection of Hugh and Dorothea Morris. Photo by Ron Behrmann.

Most of the New Mexican images of Santiago are with the horse standing still. Charlie wanted to see Santiago with more action. Inspired by an article by Joseph Winter on Santiago in New Mexico Magazine, Charlie decided to do this bulto with the horse rearing up. The hat is gessoed leather. The dress and saddle are authentic to the period. Santiago is presented larger than his horse because he is seen riding a Spanish Barb, a much smaller horse. The triple base represents the Trinity. Santiago is seen as the defender of the faith. This is one of Debbie's favorite pieces made by Charlie.

TOP: San Nicolás Obispo/Saint Nicholas the Bishop retablo, 1989. Size: 7" x 11.5". Collection of Sandra Banstorp. Photo by Ebbe Banstorp.

BOTTOM: San Nicolás Obispo retablo, 1989. Size: 6" x 8". Private Collection. Photo by Craig Varjabedian.

LEFT: San Nicolás Obispo bulto, 1990. Size: 16" tall. Charlie's research shows that most old images of bishops depicted them without a cape. Private Collection. Photo by owner.

TOP: *Nuestra Señora del Carmen retablo, 1990. Size: 5" x 10.5". Collection of Barbara and Bill Douglas. Photo by Robert Reck.*

BOTTOM: *Nuestra Señora del Carmen retablo, 1990. Size: 8" x 11". Collection of Sandra Banstorp. Photo by Ebbe Banstorp.*

RIGHT: *Nuestra Señora del Carmen bulto, 1990. Size: 19" tall. This piece was inspired by the front cover of E. Boyd's* Popular Arts of Spanish New Mexico. *Private Collection. Photo by Rey Móntez.*

This is the first and only bulto of Santa Barbara that Charlie has ever done. It was inspired by a piece by José Aragón; see George Mills' _The People of the Saints_, figure 17.

TOP: Santa Barbara retablo, 1989. Size: 7.5" x 11". Authors' Collection. Photo by Ron Behrmann.

BOTTOM: Santa Barbara retablo, 1988. Size: 8" x 11". Collection of Jennifer Martinez and William McArthur. Photo by Robert Reck.

LEFT: Santa Barbara bulto, 1988. Size: 14.5" tall. The similarity between this piece and older santos is most evident if one compares it to Mitchell Wilder and Edgar Breitenbach's _Santos, The Religious Folk Art of New Mexico_, Plate 3. Collection of Sandra Banstorp. Photo by Ebbe Banstorp.

The Lenten Story

This story was told by Charlie the first week of Lent, 1994 in his home.

I grew up understanding the New Mexican concept of Lent – long before I became involved in the morada. There are two times a year that the church focused on prayer, meditation, and a sequence of events that led up to the culmination of the season, namely Christmas with the birth and Lent with the crucifixion. As a child I always remembered the stories that went with each of the cycles.

Debbie's uncle Floyd once told me that "if you learn the alabados, the stories, you will learn the stories and lessons of your ancestors." The stories that we tell haven't changed for 50 or 100 years; they haven't changed for generations. If you listen to the stories, they deal with the cycles, sequences, the passion and death of Christ; they are all related.

The Lenten story to me begins again with Adam and Eve. There is no necessity for the crucifixion and the cleansing unless there is the birth, or if the old order is out of sync. Although we don't dwell on that part of the story, this is where the Lent cycle begins. Ash Wednesday brings us all back to Genesis – "from dust thou art; dust thou shall return." As an adult I have come to realize that the church, and we as Hispanics, always come back to the beginning. In this sense, Lent is where we all begin again.

During the Encuentro, the encounter between Christ and his Blessed Mother, there is a profound exchange that also draws us back to Adam and Eve. Christ says "Go back; go back to the waters of the Flood, to the waters of the Ark and the Covenant of Noah. Go back to the time of Adam and Eve." In other words, remove yourself back to the time when all was pure and that way you will not have to suffer the pending event of His crucifixion.

From Ash Wednesday, we jump from Adam and Eve all the way to the condemnation of Christ and all the events leading up to the Holy Week. After Ash Wednesday, every Friday during Lent is dedicated to a particular saint having to do with the crucifixion or the Passion. For instance, the Friday before Palm Sunday is the Friday of Our Lady of the Sorrows. Our Lady of Sorrows is the troubled mother, if you will, the pained mother watching her son being tormented. Everything we do is designed to remind us of the sequence of events that culminates with the crucifixion. The fourth Friday of Lent is the Friday of Our Lord Jesus of Nazarene. The fifth Friday is the Friday of Saint Peter.

There is always a reminder of why we are here as well as the sequence of events leading up to the passion and death of Christ. Traditionally, all the images in the morada focused on this – the Virgin of Sorrows, the Virgin of Solitude, Saint John the Evangelist at the foot of the cross, Saint Peter and the cock, and, of course, Christ.

Everything reflected on the passion and death of Christ. Historically in New Mexico, very little dealt with the resurrection of Christ. I only know of three retablos that show this scene. There are, however, some bultos that could have been redressed and reattributed with a white robe and crown. But that tradition seems to have been lost.

The traditional Hispanic way of looking at Catholicism and the Lenten sequence is with the Gospel of Mark – it ends with the crucifixion. All the other Gospels go through the resurrection. They don't end at the crucifixion. In Catholic Hispanic New Mexico, Lent stops with Mark and the crucifixion. The reason is that dying is the ultimate act, not the resurrection. Christ cannot be resurrected unless He is dead. He cannot save the world unless He dies. This probably comes from the long-standing suffering that Hispanic New Mexicans endured on this landscape. The hardships of colonial New Mexico caused people to constantly reflect not on the resurrection, but on the suffering of Christ. This

TOP: Last Supper retablo, 1993. Size: 15.75" x 17.75". Charlie's research has not uncovered any New Mexican renditions of the Last Supper. Charlie wanted to do this piece in a style that might have been used had a New Mexican santero done it. This is a folk Baroque style according to Charlie. Collection of Debra and Ross Hassig. Photo by owner.

BOTTOM: Santa Verónica con El Divino Rostro/Saint Veronica's Veil retablo, 1991. Size: 11" x 17". Collection of William Hart McNichols. Photo by Mary Elkins.

probably explains why New Mexican crucifixes are as bloody as any in the world. Our ancestors suffered and they understood Christ's suffering. This may be why in New Mexico the cross is always leading the procession as the *guía* or guide — except on Good Friday when the procession is led by Death. Hence the focus of Hispanic New Mexicans is on the crucifix; Christ is our guide, our way. This is a profound way of looking at the world.

TOP: La Santisima Trinidad/Holy Trinity retablo, 1987. Size: 8" x 11.5". Artist's Collection. Photo by Robert Reck.

BOTTOM: Santo Niño de Nacimiento retablo, 1986. Size: 5.5" x 6". Watercolor paints and natural pigments. Private Collection. Photo by Ron Behrmann.

LEFT: El Niño Perdido bulto, 1994. Size: 14" tall bulto. Mica window in back of nicho. The Christ Child is depicted preaching to the elders in the Temple. See William Wroth's <u>Christian Images in Hispanic New Mexico</u>, *page 156, plate 135 to compare this piece with one by José Rafael Aragón. Authors' Collection. Photo by Ron Behrmann.*

TOP: San Lorenzo retablo, 1986. Size: 6" x 10". Collection of Jennifer Martinez and William McArthur. Photo by Robert Reck.

BOTTOM: San Miguel retablo, 1994. Size: 16.25" x 18.25". Private Collection. Photo by Ron Behrmann.

RIGHT: La Santísima Trinidad gesso relief retablo, 1993. Size: 12" x 18". Exhibited as a part of the Albuquerque Museum <u>Charles M. Carrillo: Santos</u> show in 1993 to celebrate "The Year of American Craft: A Celebration of the Creative Work of the Hand." Collection of Jennifer Martinez and William McArthur. Photo by Robert Reck.

Charlie was inspired to do this piece by the "vertical trinity." Charlie started this piece as a bulto. The head of God the Father was originally going to be a bulto, but instead he was inspired to do a gesso relief. The body of the retablo is womb-like, like a Trinity Pieta, enveloped by the robe. God the Father and Christ are resting on the world with the "celestial stimulus" behind them.

✝

"During Lent is the best time to dig for the treasure because it is closer to the surface. During Lent you are also closer to God because you have been cleansed."

Father Tom Steele, S.J.

Clockwise from upper left: Santa Librada, El Espíritu Santo/The Holy Spirit or the Dove, San Acacio, Arma Cristi/Implements of the Passion, San Ignacio de Loyola, San Francisco de Asís, San Juan Nepomuceno, El Sagrador Corazón y las Cinco Llagas/The Sacred Heart and the Five Wounds, and in the center Nuestro Señor de Esquípulas.

TOP : San Calletano/Saint Gaetano retablo, 1988. Size: 10" x 14". The inspirartion for this piece is by Rafael Aragón. See E. Boyd's Popular Arts of Spanish New Mexico, page 414, plate 35, José Espinosa's Saints in the Valleys, page 43, plate 19 and Robin Farwell Gavins' Traditional Arts of Spanish New Mexico, page 38. Private Collection. Photo by artist.

LEFT: Muestras para la Hermandad/Patterns of the Brotherhood retablo, 1993. Size: 14" x 19". Commissioned for En Divina Luz: The Penitente Moradas of New Mexico and its accompanying travelling exhibition from The Albuquerque Museum. Private Collection. Photo by Craig Varjabedian.

TOP: *Nuestra Señora retablo*, 1986. Size: 4.75" x 10". This is very reminiscent of a piece by José Rafael Aragón. See E. Boyd's *Popular Arts of Spanish New Mexico*, page 415, plate 36. Private Collection. Photo by artist.

RIGHT: *Nuestra Señora de los Dolores bulto*, 1993. Size: 11" tall. Exhibited as a part of Albuquerque Museum *1994 Miniatures Show*. Authors' Collection. Photo by Robert Reck.

Charlie wanted to make a simple bulto reminiscent of a small home-style devotional piece. The body of this bulto is all one piece of wood, except for the gessoed hands. The inspiration for this piece came from the Arroyo Hondo Santero; see Larry Frank's *New Kingdom of the Saints*, plate 232, William Worth's *Christian Images in Hispanic New Mexico*, page 187, plate 177 and Robin Farwell Gavins' *Traditional Arts of Spanish New Mexico*, page 45.

The body of this bulto is all one piece of wood. The inspiration for this piece was from the Arroyo Hondo Santero; see Larry Frank's New Kingdom of the Saints, plate 232, William Worth's Christian Images in Hispanic New Mexico, page 187, plate 177 and Robin Farwell Gavins' Traditional Arts of Spanish New Mexico, page 45.

TOP: Nuestra Señora de la Manga, Abogada de los Partos/Our Lady of the Sleeve, Advocate of Childbirth retablo, 1991. Size: 11.75" x 17". This is a New Mexican variation of Nuestra Señora de los Dolores. Private Collection. Photo by Craig Varjabedian.

LEFT: Nuestra Señora de los Dolores bulto, 1994. Size: 10" tall. Private Collection. Photo by Ron Behrmann.

†

The Seven Sorrows

Although there are at least three different versions of the seven sorrows, the standard seven as known in colonial New Mexico are as follows:

1. *The Circumcision*
2. *The Flight into Egypt*
3. *The Child Lost in the Temple*
4. *The Encounter of the Virgin and Christ*
5. *The Nailing of Christ/the Crucifixion*
6. *The Descent from the Cross*
7. *The Entombment of Christ*

The bulto of Nuestra Señora de los Siete Dolores is depicted with seven daggers, one for each of the sorrows.

RIGHT: Nuestra Señora de los Siete Dolores/Soledad bulto, 1991. Cottonwood root, pine, canvas, gesso, natural pigments, varnish, tin. Size: 44" x 22.5" x 11". Winner of the E. Boyd Memorial Award for originality and expressive design at the 1991 Spanish Market. Cover piece for ¡Chispas! Cultural Warriors of New Mexico catalog and part of ¡Chispas! traveling exhibit. The source for this bulto was an Our Lady hollowframe by the Santo Niño Santero. See E. Boyd's Popular Arts of Spanish New Mexico, page 380, plate 199. Collection of The Heard Museum. Photo by Craig Smith courtesy of The Heard Museum, Phoenix, Ariz.

TOP: *Nuestra Señora de los Dolores retablo*, 1988. Size: 11" x 16". Collection of Jennifer Martinez and William McArthur. Photo by Robert Reck.

BOTTOM: *Nuestra Señora de Guadalupe retablo*, 1987. Size: 10" x 13". Private Collection. Photo by Kirk Gittings.

LEFT: *Nuestra Señora de los Siete Dolores bulto*, 1992. Size: 47.5" tall; 8.5" tall repisa. Collection of Mr. and Mrs. H. Earl Hoover II. Photo by Ron Behrmann.

TOP: San Pedro/Saint Peter retablo, 1994. Size: 8" x 11.25". Private Collection. Photo by Ron Behrmann.

BOTTOM: San Pedro/Saint Peter retablo, 1986. Size: 5.5" x 11". Watercolor paints. Private Collection. Photo by artist.

RIGHT: San Geronimo/Saint Jerome retablo with gesso relief, 1992. Size: 19.5" x 28". First Place retablo in 1992 Spanish Market. Collection of JoAnn and Robert Balzer. Photo by Robert Reck.

Charlie had completed a number of small gesso relief pieces and he was not very inspired by their results. Using those as a learning experience, he wanted to push the medium. This piece was the first gesso relief retablo to win a Spanish Market award. This retablo contains the standard iconography for Jerome, except for the column and ink well/quill pen. The column is allegorical of Jerome doing penance and flagellation. The rock in his left hand and the column represent the pillar of Christ. This retablo has a Laguna-style border.

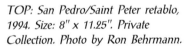

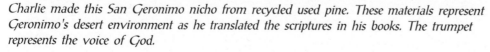

Charlie made this San Geronimo nicho from recycled used pine. These materials represent Geronimo's desert environment as he translated the scriptures in his books. The trumpet represents the voice of God.

TOP: San Geronimo retablo, 1984. Size: 3" x 4.5". Watercolor paints. Private Collection. Photo by Ron Behrmann.

BOTTOM: San Vicente de Saragosa retablo, 1989. Size: 9" x 18". Collection of Betty Stewart. Photo by Ebbe Banstorp.

LEFT: San Geronimo bulto, 1992. Size: 10" tall bulto; 17" tall honoria. Collection of Nancy Clark Reynolds. Photo by Robert Reck.

†

TOP: Santa Rita retablo, 1991. Size: 9" x 12". Private Collection. Photo by Craig Varjabedian.

BOTTOM: Nuestra Señora de Guadalupe retablo, 1992. Size: 14" x 18". Private Collection. Photo by Craig Varjabedian.

RIGHT: Nuestra Señora de los Dolores bulto, 1988. Size: 38" tall. Charlie wanted to make a dressable Virgin – a bulto de vestir – which is why this piece has moveable arms. The size of this piece was inspired by a bulto of Our Lady in Abiquiú. The face of this bulto resembles Debbie's mother, Louisa. Artist's Collection. Photo by Rey Móntez.

TOP: Cristatado a la Columna/ Christ at the Column retablo, 1990. (La Fagelación del Señor/Cristo Azotado). Size: 7" x 10". See William Wroth's Christian Images in Hispanic New Mexico, page 149, plate 124 for a piece by José Rafael Aragón that is strikingly similar. Private Collection. Photo by Ron Behrmann.

LEFT: Cristo a la Columna/Christ at the Column bulto, 1992. Size: 27" tall. Because of Christ's wounds, this was one of the most emotionally challenging pieces for Charlie to make. See George Mills' The People of the Saints, figure 1 and William Wroth's Images of Penance, Images of Mercy, page 122, plates 57 and 58. Exhibited as a part of the Albuquerque Museum Charles M. Carrillo: Santos show in 1993 to celebrate "The Year of American Craft: A Celebration of the Creative Work of the Hand." Collection of Ramón and Nance Lopéz. Photo by Robert Reck.

Via Crucis/Stations of the Way of the Cross

The Via Crucis as described by the Penitente Brothers are as follows:

1. *Jesús condenado á muerte* (Christ condemned to death by Pilate)
2. *Jesús con la cruz a cuestas* (Jesus is made to carry the cross)
3. *Jesús cae primera vez* (Jesus falls the first time)
4. *Jesús encuentra á su santisima Madre* (Jesus meets his blessed Mother)
5. *Jesús ayudado por el Cireneo á llevar la cruz* (The cross is laid on Simon of Cyrene)
6. *La Verónica limpia el rostro á Jesús* (Veronica wipes the face of Jesus)
7. *Jesús cae por segunda vez* (Jesus falls the second time)
8. *Jesús consuela á las mujeres de Jerusalén* (Jesus speaks to the women of Jerusalem)
9. *Jesús cae por tercera vez* (Jesus falls the third time)
10. *Desnudan á Jesús y le dan á beber hiel* (Jesus is stripped of his garments and receives gall to drink)
11. *Jesús es clavado en la cruz* (Jesus is nailed to the cross)
12. *Jesús muere en la cruz* (Jesus dies on the cross)
13. *Jesús bajado de la cruz, es puesto en los brazos de su santísima Madre* (Jesus is taken down from the cross)
14. *Jesús es sepultado* (Jesus is laid in the sepulcher)

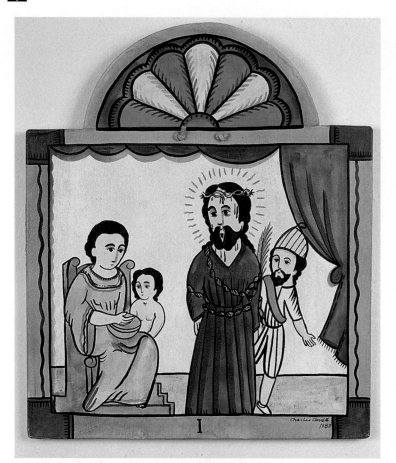

TOP RIGHT: Jesús condenado á muerte: The First Station of the Way of the Cross, 1987. Size: 11" x 13.5". Archdiocese of Santa Fe Chapel. Photo by Ron Behrmann.

BOTTOM RIGHT: Jesús es clavado en la cruz: The Eleventh Station of the Way of the Cross, 1987. Size: 11" x 13.5". Archdiocese of Santa Fe Chapel. Photo by Ron Behrmann.

Byzantine Saints & Holy Days

All Souls

Celebrated the first Saturday before Lent, the second, third and fourth Saturday of Lent, and the Saturday before Pentecost. This is the commemoration of all the departed; after a liturgy requiem service (Panachida) all the dead of the parish are remembered by name. The retablo, based on a fresco at St. Catherine's at Mt. Sinai, shows Abraham leading souls into Paradise.

Our Lady of the Sign

Celebrated before Christmas. This retablo shows the Virgin Mary with hands extended in prayer (Orans) with Christ incarnate in her womb. Christ is a small man holding the scroll, a symbol of God's eternal word.

Trinity

Celebrated the Monday after Pentecost. This retablo, based on the St. Andrew Rublev icon, is from Genesis showing the three angels and the revelation of the Holy Trinity.

TOP: LEFT: All Souls retablo, 1986. Size: 8" x 11". Watercolor paints and natural pigments. Our Lady of Perpetual Help Byzantine Catholic Church, Albuquerque. Photo by Ron Behrmann.

TOP RIGHT: Our Lady of the Sign retablo, 1986. Size: 8" x 11". Watercolor paints and natural pigments. Our Lady of Perpetual Help Byzantine Catholic Church, Albuquerque. Photo by Ron Behrmann.

BOTTOM RIGHT: Old Testament Trinity or Hospitality of Abraham retablo, 1986. Size: 8" x 11". Watercolor paints and natural pigments. Our Lady of Perpetual Help Byzantine Catholic Church, Albuquerque. Photo by Ron Behrmann.

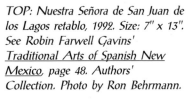

TOP: Nuestra Señora de San Juan de los Lagos retablo, 1992. Size: 7" x 13". See Robin Farwell Gavins' Traditional Arts of Spanish New Mexico, page 48. Authors' Collection. Photo by Ron Behrmann.

BOTTOM: Nuestra Señora de San Juan de los Lagos retablo, 1987. Size: 8" x 10". Watercolor paints. Collection of Alexandra Rhetts. Photo by Ron Behrmann.

RIGHT: Nuestra Señora de los Dolores retablo, 1991. Size: 6" x 9". Authors' Collection. Photo by Ron Behrmann.

Charlie had been doing a lot of research at the Museum of International Folk Art in Santa Fe and had been looking at several similar masterpieces for devotion by the Laguna Santero. Charlie has not done very many pieces with the frame found in this piece. See E. Boyd's Popular Arts of Spanish New Mexico, page 146, Figure 110 and Robin Farwell Gavin's Traditional Arts of Spanish New Mexico, page 74. Charlie was also influenced by several pieces by the Laguna Santero in the Museum collection. Charlie's smaller pieces are just wonderful; he says that they take more time to do than bigger ones.

TOP: *Nuestra Señora de San Juan de los Lagos retablo,* 1993. Size: 13.5" x 25". Exhibited as a part of the *¡Chispas!* show at the Heard Museum. Private Collection. Photo by Ron Behrmann.

BOTTOM: *Nuestra Señora de San Juan de los Lagos retablo,* 1993. Size: 6" x 9". Collection of Betty Stewart. Photo by Ebbe Banstorp.

LEFT: *Nuestra Señora de San Juan de los Lagos bulto,* 1994. Size: 16.5" tall. Private Collection. Photo by Ron Behrmann.

TOP: *Santa Gertrudis retablo, 1986. Size: 5.5" x 7". Collection of Jennifer Martinez and William McArthur. Photo by Robert Reck.*

BOTTOM: *San Nicolás Obispo retablo, 1991. Size: 6" x 9". Collection of Jennifer Martinez and William McArthur. Photo by Robert Reck.*

RIGHT: *San Felipe de Jesús bulto, 1993. Size: 19.5" tall. Exhibited as a part of the Albuquerque Museum* <u>Charles M. Carrillo: Santos</u> *show in 1993 to celebrate "The Year of American Craft: A Celebration of the Creative Work of the Hand." Collection of the Albuquerque Museum, purchase/donation from 1991 General Obligation Bonds and Gift of Nancy Pletka (93.048.002). Photo by Robert Reck.*

There are many nice Mexican versions of San Felipe de Jesús. Charlie was inspired to do this piece by the photos in <u>Mexico: Splendor of Thirty Centuries</u>, plate 325. The spears are symbolic of a Japanese style of execution.

Santos/Saints

This section is designed to provide additional information to our readers about the pieces contained in this book. We have attempted to provide an explanation of every santo/saint created by Charlie Carrillo and displayed in this book.

San Acacio/Saint Acacius of Mount Ararat

Feast Day - June 22. Patron of those who experience crucifixion and military protector against any intruders. 2nd Century. Leader of Roman soldiers. Converted to Christianity and crucified. Venerated in Northern New Mexico. Usually seen bearded and flanked on the cross by two or more soldiers.

San Andres/Saint Andrew

Feast Day - November 30. Patron of fishermen, sailors, and spinsters. Also seen as the Patron of Greece, Russia, Scotland. Invoked against gout and neck problems. A fisherman, he was a follower of John the Baptist and later became a disciple of Jesus. He was the brother of Peter. He was crucified on an x-shaped cross for baptizing the wife of the Roman governor of Patras.

San Antonio de Padua/Saint Anthony

Feast Day - June 13. Patron of lost objects, for finding a worthy husband, for women who want children, finding a fortune. He is also a patron of cattle and burros. 1195-1232. Anthony is popular in folklore for being able to talk to animals. It may have come from the story that he was a student of San Francisco. He is also useful in homes for finding lost objects. Born in Lisbon, he is sometimes seen in a Franciscan blue (blue for Mary) robe with a cord tie, holding a book. Sometimes the Christ child is sitting on the book and Anthony is tonsured and unbearded.

San Antonio Abad/Saint Anthony

Feast Day — January 17. Patron of domesticated animals. He was a great abbot and spiritual guide of the monasteries of Egypt in the 3rd Century. It was customary in Spanish Colonial times to bless farm animals of his feast day.

Santa Bárbara/Saint Barbara

Feast Day - December 4. Patron of miners, artillery men, firemen, against being struck by lightning. 200 or 300 AD. Daughter of a pagan from Nicomedia, she was imprisoned in a tower to discourage suitors. While imprisoned, she became a Christian, which angered her father. He beheaded her and was himself struck by lightening. New Mexican versions show her in a three-tiered dress, in front of a tower with three windows. In the background is a thundercloud and lightning bolt. She holds a palm frond. All "threes" represent the Holy Trinity.

San Bartolomeo/Saint Bartholemew or Nathaniel

Feast Day - August 24. Patron of women in childbirth, against horrible deaths and lightning. He died from what could have been a whipping or caning. He wears a red robe and prays kneeling to a cross.

"A cada Santo su función/Each Saint has his day."

New Mexican dicho

TOP: San Antonio de Padua retablo, 1993. Size: 10" x 13.25". Collection of Betty Stewart. Photo by Ebbe Banstorp.

BOTTOM: San Bartolomeo retablo, 1988. Size: 6" x 8.5". Collection of Jennifer Martinez and William McArthur. Photo by Robert Reck.

Cristo Crucificado/The Crucifixion of Christ

Celebrated on Good Friday. Christ crucified can be portrayed just on a cross or in a scene with the Virgin Mary and San Juan Evangelista, known as a Calvario (for Mt. Calvary).

Cristo a la Columna/ Christ at the Column

Before Christ was crucified, Pontius Pilate ordered his scourging at a column.

La Divina Pastora/The Divine Shepherdess

Depicted as the seated Virgin, holding lambs or sheep. Dressed in colonial garb, rounded hat. She is frequently seen holding a rose.

San Felipe de Jesús/Saint Phillip

Feast Day - February 5. Patron of Mexico City and of San Felipe Pueblo (NM). A Mexico City native who became a Franciscan. Travelled to the Philippines then to Japan where he was martyred. Wears Franciscan robes, blue, with crossed lances or swords through his torso. Many saints wear blue in honor of the Virgin Mary.

San Francisco de Asís/Saint Francis of Assisi

Feast Day - October 4. Patron – ecology, small animals, kindness, children, New Mexico and Santa Fe. 1182-1226. He left a wealthy family by direction of a vision to renounce all worldly possessions and to have a life of poverty and devotion. He founded the order of the Franciscans. Depicted in a long grey or blue habit with a cowl and capuche, with a knotted cord belt around his waist. He is bearded and tonsured with the stigmata of Christ. Associated symbols include a cross and skull; the skull is a reminder that there is life hereafter.

San Gerónimo/Saint Jerome

Feast Day - September 30. Patron of orphans and Taos Pueblo and against lightening. 342-420. Jerome is depicted in New Mexico as a Penitente hermit wearing either a long red robe or nothing. He is alone in the desert, striking his breast with a sharp rock. He prays to God, kneeling before a cross or holding one. God's voice is symbolized as a trumpet from heaven. A peaceful lion suggests how a religious order represents a return to the Garden of Eden as well as strength and knowledge. In Europe, Jerome is seen as a scholar.

Santa Gertrudis/Saint Gertrude

Feast Day - November 16. Patroness of students, educators, mystics, of the West Indies of which New Mexico was considered part, and of the Sacred Heart. 1256-1302. Gertrude was a German mystic who gave up her love of studies to worship Christ and the image of his heart. She is seen as a Benedictine nun wearing a full, black robe and carrying a staff. In her other hand she carries a heart that may be surrounded by thorns.

TOP: San Jorge/Saint George retablo, 1991. Size: 7.75" x 14.5". Private Collection. Photo by Craig Varjabedian.

BOTTOM: San Ignacio de Loyola retablo, 1991. Size: 7" x 13.25". Collection of William Hart McNichols. Photo by Mary Elkins.

La Huida a Egipto/Flight Into Egypt

Feast Day - February 17. Joseph sees in a dream that King Herod is looking for the Christ Child to kill him as a threat to his kingdom. Joseph, Mary and the Child flee to Egypt with a donkey. Sometimes angels will appear in the scene. This story is taken from the Gospel according to Saint Matthew.

San Ignacio de Loyola/Saint Ignatius Loyola

Feast Day - July 31. Patron of the Jesuits and The Brothers of Our Father Jesus the Nazarene/The Penitente Brothers see him as a mentor. 1491-1556. Founded the Society of Jesus/Jesuits. A Basque soldier who was severely wounded and became a priest. Is pictured either standing with an open book inscribed AMDG (Ad Majorem Dei Gloriam) and IHS that could be on a banner or disk or kneeling at mass with clerical vestments and a chasuble. He also can be pictured in simpler black Jesuit garb with a sash, rosary, and biretta.

Santa Inés del Campo/Saint Agnes

Feast Day - January 21. Patron of shepherds and farmers. Inés was from a noble Roman family of the late 3rd or early 4th Century. Martyred first by being burned alive and then decapitated. Her name is derived from *agnus* which means lamb. She is depicted holding a lamb because of the legend that she appeared with Jesus as the Divine Lamb after her death.

San Isidro Labradór/Saint Isidore the Farmer

Feast Day - May 15. Patron of gardeners, farmers, laborers, shepherds, and land deals. Died 1170. Isidro was a laborer for Juan de Vargas, a lord near Madrid, and an ancestor of Don Diego de Vargas, who settled New Mexico. God rewarded him, as a very holy man, by sending an angel to help with the plowing. To get a drink of water for his master, Isidro struck the ground with a gourd and an eternal spring came forth. He is pictured with an angel and oxen with plow. In New Mexico, he is seen wearing clothing of an 18th Century gentleman with wide brim hat and a staff. Along with his wife Santa María Toribia de la Cabeza, he is the patron saint of Madrid. He is frequently invoked against tempest, drought, and pests.

Jesús Nazareno/Jesus of Nazarene

A standing Jesus with loincloth and with long hair. He may be bearded and wears a crown of thorns. When the figure is large, it may have supports under the arms which may be jointed for movement. He may be wearing a red or purple robe with his hands tied in front with sinew. He may have a large stand or andas to which he is attached. A very important Penitente figure for Holy Week.

San Jorge/ Saint George

Patron of England. Popular during the Middle Ages. George is depicted as the dragon slayer. He is usually seen on a white horse directing a lance at a winged dragon on the ground below him. Saint George is not used very often in New Mexican santos.

San José Patriarca/Saint Joseph

Feast Day - March 19 (near vernal equinox). Patron – Fathers, carpenters, builders, the home, laborers, families and a happy death (Christ is traditionally believed to have been with him at death); he is the ideal saint, man, husband, and was popularly invoked for a number of circumstances. Joseph is the husband of Mary and earthly father of Christ. He was a carpenter and builder. He has a dark beard and hair, and carries a staff with flowers coming from the top. He was selected as Mary's husband by the holy men because of his flowering staff. He is pictured carrying the Christ in one hand or seated on his arm. He has a flowered robe and usually a crown. Saint Joseph is one of Charlie's favorite saints because of his roles as a husband,

TOP: Santa Librada retablo, 1988. Size: 5.75" x 11". Private Collection. Photo by artist.

BOTTOM: San Luís Gonzaga (Aloysius) retablo, 1991. Size: 8.5" x 14". Collection of William Hart McNichols. Photo by Mary Elkins.

father, and carpenter who supported his family. In New Mexico, shown as a younger man with dark beard and dark hair. Sometimes seen with carpenter's tools.

San Juan Evangelista/Saint John the Divine (or Evangelist)
Feast Day - December 27. John is said to have lived into the 2nd Century. He is shown beardless, holding a book, and perhaps wringing his hands.

San Juan Nepomuceno/Saint John Nepomuk
Feast Day - May 16. Patron of irrigation, lawyers, secrecy and against gossip and slander. 1340-1393. John Nepomuk was drowned by King Wenceslaus for not breaking the confessional vow of silence disclosing what was told him by the queen. He is shown in classic monk style with black cassock holding a palm and crucifix. Especially significant to the Penitentes for secrecy.

Santa Librada/Saint Liberata
Feast Day - July 20. Patron of liberated women. Wholly legendary. Liberata was the daughter of a pagan Portuguese king who promised her in marriage to the king of Sicily. Liberata had already decided to spend her life in devotion to Christ and prayed to be disfigured so that the marriage would not happen. God answered her prayers and caused her to grow a beard. Her father crucified her in anger. In New Mexico she is thought of as the Penitente saint for women — a female counterpart to Christ and his crucifixion.

San Lorenzo/Saint Lorenzo
Feast Day - August 10. Patron of the poor and of August crops and against fire. Lorenzo, a Spanish deacon in service to the Pope, was burned alive. He is shown in deacon's robes holding either a book, chalice, palm, or a grid-iron. Lorenzo is usually tonsured and beardless.

San Luís Gonzaga/Saint Aloysius Gonzaga
Feast Day - June 21 (summer solstice). Patron of boys and invoked by pregnant women. 1568-1591. Son of a Venice nobleman, he joined the Jesuit novitiate against his father's wishes. Died six years later from the plague in Rome, contracted while working with the sick. Pictured wearing a white surplice over a black cassock with collar. He has no facial hair and carries a crucifix and lilies.

Santa María Magdalena/Mary Magdalene
Feast Day - July 22. Patroness of women and converts. Usually shown at the foot of the cross. A woman of questionable background whom Christ converted. She is shown in a long green gown and red cloak. She is an important part of the Lenten story and is prayed to on Good Friday.

Santa María Toribia de la Cabeza/Saint Mary
See also San Isidro. With her husband San Isidro, she is the patron saint of Madrid. She is invoked when dealing with bad neighbors.

San Miguel Arcángel/Saint Michael the Archangel
Feast Day - May 8 and September 29 (just after autumnal equinox). Patron of those who are ill, police, soldiers, radiologists, defender of faith, lawyers, against all evil; protector of the Church; he is invoked during temptations

TOP: San José retablo, 1989. Size: 8" x 13". Collection of Betty Stewart. Photo by Ebbe Banstorp.

BOTTOM: San Juan Nepomuceno retablo, 1988. Size: 5.5" x 8". See Robin Farwell Gavins' Traditional Arts of Spanish New Mexico, page 81. Collection of Jennifer Martinez and William McArthur. Photo by Robert Reck.

and at the time of death. Michael, the most important of angels (his name means "Who is like God"), is winged and equipped with a sword to conquer the forces of evil. He holds the scales of judgement as Lord of Souls. His duties include weighing the deeds done in life by the deceased and recommending heaven, purgatory, or hell.

San Nicolás Obispo/Saint Nicholas of Myra

Feast Day - December 6. Patron of a peaceful death, children and marriageable girls. Died 350. Nicholas is dressed as a bishop in a cape, with beard, holding a palm and dove – sometimes in a shell. He can also hold a staff or book. Nicholas is famous for good deeds and miracles.

Santo Niño de Atocha/Holy Child

Feast Day - Christmas. Patron of politicians and political prisoners and against sudden misfortune. The Santo Niño de Atocha originated in Plateros, Mexico, and the story traveled north into New Mexico. He is usually seated and dressed as a pilgrim or contemporary clothing, holding a staff and a water container. Usually in the picture are a basket and leg irons. He has several different stories with the original taking place in prisons where he fed the imprisoned. In New Mexico he was associated with healing powers, especially at Chimayó. He is said to wander the fields at night performing good deeds while wearing out his shoes, which people leave for him.

Santo Niño/Infant Christ

Feast Day - Christmas. Patron of children, of the sick, of travelers. Can be represented by himself, sitting or being held by the Virgin, San José, or Saint Anthony. Other versions of the Christ Child include: Niño Perdido or lost Christ Child, a standing figure in a loincloth; Niño Praga, holding a globe with a cross on top, usually in a red robe; Niño Alma, floating in air, usually wearing a white robe and with star or stars in the background; or Nacimiento, just born.

Nuestro Señor de Esquipilas/Our Lord of Esquipilas

During the 1800s when the Santuario of Chimayó was constructed, this Guatemalan image was brought to the Chimayó area. The crucifix and the tree of life become one in the image. It is representative of sacred earth which is consistent with the Chimayó legend.

Nuestra Señora de la Asunción/Our Lady of the Assumption

Feast Day - August 15. Mary rises into heaven in body and soul.

Nuestra Señora del Carmen/Our Lady of Mount Carmel

Feast Day - July 18. The Virgin of Mount Carmel is crowned and dressed with a cream colored outer robe or cape over the Carmelite Order brown robe. She is standing and may hold the Christ. She can intervene on behalf of souls in purgatory.

TOP: Nuestra Señora del Carmen retablo, 1992. Size: 9" x 13". Private Collection. Photo by Ron Behrmann.

BOTTOM: Nuestra Señora de Guadalupe con Santo Entierro/Santo Sepultado retablo, 1989. Size" 8.5" x 20". See Thomas Steele's Santos and Saints, page 42 for the inspiration for this piece. Private Collection. Photo by Craig Varjabedian.

Nuestra Señora de Guadalupe/Our Lady of Guadalupe

Feast Day - December 12 (near winter solstice). Patron of the Americas, especially Native Americans and Hispanic peoples, also against all evil, war, and ills. In New Mexico, she is considered the ideal woman, wife, and mother. Nuestra Señora de Guadalupe is the most recognized image of the Virgin. She has been the patron of Mexico since 1531. At that time she is

reported to have appeared to the Indian Juan Diego at Tepeyac in Mexico City. She asked him to tell the bishop to build a shrine in her honor. Of course, the bishop needed further convincing and asked for a sign. When Juan Diego returned to the original site, the vision of Mary reappeared. She told Juan Diego to take back to the bishop fresh roses that miraculously appeared all around her on the hillside. It was the middle of winter. The Virgin arranged the roses in Juan Diego's cloak. When the cloak was presented to the bishop, the roses fell to the floor and the image of Mary appeared on the cloth. Our Lady of Guadalupe is usually pictured wearing a turquoise blue mantle with stars and a halo of yellow sunlike rays, and standing on a black crescent moon which is held up by a small angel.

Nuestra Señora de la Luz/Our Lady of Light

Feast Day - May 21. Patroness of those returning to the Church and estranged husbands. Also wisdom gained by the light of education and salvation from hell and purgatory. Mary is pictured with Christ and is saving a soul from the devil or hell. An angel may be present.

Nuestra Señora de la Purísima or Imaculada Concepción/Our Lady of the Immaculate Conception

Feast Day - December 8. From the moment of her conception in the womb of her mother Ann, Mary is believed to have been without original sin. The moon and 12 stars represent Revelations 12:1. There are many versions of the Immaculate Conception in New Mexico, most of which show her as a young woman cloaked in a blue mantle and red dress with hands in prayer.

Nuestra Señora de Refugio de Pecadores/Our Lady Refuge of Sinners

This image came to New Mexico through introduction in Mexico by Jesuits. She is shown with Christ as a child standing on her knee and occasionally holding her thumb. They are enthroned on a cloud. She is shown with a blue mantle and a white scarf and both are wearing crowns.

Nuestra Señora del Rosario/Our Lady of the Rosary

Feast Day - October 7. Patroness of peace and against danger and accidents. She is also prayed to with the rosary for acceptance of death. Mary wearing a blue robe with a mantle draped across her left arm. She is standing. There is a crescent moon at her feet or on the bottom of her dress, and she holds Christ. Sometimes wearing a red dress under the blue robe and may be holding a rosary. One version of Our Lady of the Rosary is La Conquistadora in the Saint Francis Cathedral in Santa Fe. The image itself is surrounded by controversy since it is associated with the Pueblo Revolt of 1680 and the Reconquest of 1692-93. She is part of the Santa Fe Fiesta celebration held in Santa Fe in early September.

Nuestra Señora de San Juan de los Lagos/Our Lady of St, John of the Lakes

Feast Day - February 2. San Juan de Los Lagos is a small town north of Mexico City. It is noted for its famous statue of Mary. A copy of the image was brought to New Mexico (Talpa) in the early 1800s by settlers.

Nuestra Señora de los Siete Dolores/Our Lady of the Seven Sorrows or Nuestra Señora de los Dolores/Our Lady of Sorrows

Feast Day - Friday before Palm Sunday and September 16. Patroness of chil-

TOP: San Pascual Bailón retablo, 1991. Size: 7" x 10.5" Collection of Santa Fe artist Robert Stevens. Photo by Robert Reck.

BOTTOM: San Ramón Nonato/Saint Raymond Nonatus retablo, 1991. Size: 7.25" x 10". Collection of Santa Fe artist Robert Stevens. Photo by Craig Varjabedian.

dren, women in childbirth, compassion, and sinners. She is very plainly dressed in a long red mantle over tunic. She is wringing her hands over the crucifixion of her son and stands at the foot of his cross or has one or seven daggers in her heart to represent the seven sorrows. The sword(s), red/blue tunic, and possible crown make her different from Nuestra Señora de Soledad/Our Lady of Solitude. A Penitente figure. The most often used image in New Mexico, there are forty-seven churches in New Mexico named for her.

San Pascual Bailón/Saint Pascual

Feast Day - May 17. Patron of sheep, shepherds, and cooks. 1540-1592. Pascual was a shepherd from Aragón who became a Franciscan. He led a very humble life and was distinguished for his devotion to the Most Holy Eucharist. He is often depicted with a monstrance or chalice in his hand or in homage to the Holy Eucharist. He is also pictured with a lamb and shepherd's staff. He is considered patron of cooks because of the legend that his kitchen duties were miraculously taken care of while he prayed before the Blessed Sacrament.

San Pedro Apostol/Saint Peter the Apostle

Feast Day - June 29. Patron of a happy death with entrance into heaven, freedom for prisoners, church unity and against fevers. Peter was the leader of the apostles and the first pope of the Church. He is pictured as the keeper of the gates of heaven, in a long robe, wearing a beard. He carries a key or two and may be carrying a book.

San Rafael Arcángel/Saint Raphael the Archangel

Feast Day - October 24. Patron of fishermen, friendship, happy meetings, good health and marriage, against blindness. Guide for travelers and pilgrims. Shown or depicted as a winged angel usually dressed in red, sometimes wearing a crown of roses. Always shown with a traveler's staff from which hangs a gourd or water bottle. In the opposite hand Rafael holds a fish. In New Mexico, this is often a cutthroat or a rainbow trout.

San Ramón Nonato/Saint Raymond Nonatus

Feast Day - August 31. Patron of pregnant women, the unborn, secrecy for Penitentes, against curses and slander. Died 1240. A member of the order of N.S. de la Merced, he volunteered himself into slavery to free prisoners of the Moors. He refused to stop preaching while in captivity and his lips were pierced with a red-hot iron and padlocked. He was later released and became a cardinal. He is pictured wearing a red or orange chasuble over white robes, holds a monstrance and a wand with three crowns. He is often bearded.

TOP: Santa Gertrudis/Saint Gertrude retablo, 1991. Milled lumber. Size: 11.75" x 16". Private Collection. Photo by Craig Varjabedian.

BOTTOM: La Sagrada Familia/The Holy Family retablo, 1990. Milled lumber. Size: 11.75" x 16". This image was inspired by the works of José Aragón and José Rafael Aragón. See Thomas Steele's Santos and Saints, page 120 and William Wroth's Christian Images in Hispanic New Mexico, page 112, plate 75. Private Collection. Photo by Craig Varjabedian.

Relicario/Reliquary

Relics of saints, their possessions, or things they used or touched are kept in containers for devotion. They may be highly ornamented or plain.

Santa Rita de Casia/Saint Rita of Cascia

Feast Day - May 22. 1381-1457. Patroness of desperate cases and keeps husbands faithful. Depicted as a young woman dressed in the black robes of the Augustinian nuns, she was married against her will in accordance to her parents' wishes. As a widow she became a nun. While meditating a thorn from Christ was implanted in her forehead so she could suffer with Christ.

La Sagrada Familia/The Holy Family

Feast Day - First Sunday after January 6. Patrons of families, travelers and refugees. The trio of Jesus, the Virgin Mary, and Joseph is an earthly correlative of the Eternal Trinity. In La Sagrada Familia, the Child is usually in the center holding his parents' hands. The story is taken from the Gospel according to Saint Matthew.

Santiago/Saint James

Feast Day - July 25. Patron of Spain, warriors, horsemen, horses, and military. Saint James is portrayed on a white horse (Caballero) and becomes a conqueror of the Moors (Matamoros). It is reported that James was the brother of John the Evangelist and that a king had a vision of James in a dream promising help from God in the war with the Moors. He became a symbol of courage in battle.

La Santísma Trinidád/The Holy Trinity

Feast Day - Sunday after Pentecost. For all favors, deliverance from beasts, earthquakes, and famine. The three figures are God the Father, God the Son, and God the Holy Ghost or Spirit. Usually depicted in a horizontal line as three bearded men with triangular halos or the Spirit can appear as a dove. All wear long robes with the Father (center figure) given the New Mexican symbolism of crown, sun and scepter, the Son or Christ (figure on right), with a lamb, and The Holy Spirit (usually seen on the left with a dove). They are frequently seen holding a rope or chain which represents their unity.

Doña Sebastiana, La Carreta, Muerte, El Angel de Muerte/Death Cart or Death Figure

A Penitente processional image who is a fearful reminder rather than an image for reverence. The figure on the cart is seductive yet skeletal and horrible. She is often depicted with a long braid of grey hair, usually wearing a black cape, and may be carrying a bow and arrow that is threatening a swift death to the procession, or an ax or hatchet for a slow death.

Santa Teresa de Ávila/Saint Theresa of Avila

Feast Day - October 15. Patron of pilots, aviation and mystics, and against headaches. 1515-1582. Founder of the Discalced Carmelites. Teresa is dressed in nun's garb with an emblem, holding a crucifix and palm. She is associated with the Good Friday drama.

TOP: La Huida a Egipto/Flight into Egypt retablo, 1988. Size: 9.75" x 20". Private Collection. Photo by Craig Varjabedian.

BOTTOM: Santa Barbara retablo, 1990. Size: 6.75" x 14". Private Collection. Photo by Craig Varjabedian.

Santa Verónica/Saint Veronica

Feast Day - Good Friday. 6th Station of the Way of the Cross. Shown as a nun who holds a handkerchief or veil imprinted with the face of Christ. Some see Veronica as a version of the Virgin Mary.

San Vicente Ferrer/Saint Vincent Ferrer

Feast Day - April 5. Patron of charity and wine growers. 1350-1400. A Dominican brother who is said to have had miraculous powers. He is shown with wings, holding a cross with a rosary and a skull in the background. He is a Penitente saint.

TOP: *Cristo Crucificado/Christ Crucified retablo with gesso relief, 1988. Size: 18.5 x 24.5". Christ's head, loin cloth and blood are in relief. Silk ribbons extend from the wounds. Collection of the Museum of International Folk Art, Santa Fe. Photo by artist.*

BOTTOM: *Cristo Crucificado/ Christ Crucified bulto, 1991. Size: 12" x 18". Private Collection. Photo by Rudy Miera.*

LEFT: *Cristo Crucificado/Christ Crucified bulto, 1994. Size: 12" x 23.5". The source for this piece was probably José Rafael Aragón. See Larry Frank's* New Kingdom of the Saints, *page 240, plate 226. Collection of Al & Beverlee Richter. Photo by Ron Behrmann.*

TOP: La Santisima Trinidad/The Holy Trinity retablo, 1985. Size: 4" x 5.5". Watercolor paints. Artist's Collection. Photo by Robert Reck.

BOTTOM: La Santisima Trinidad retablo, 1983. Size: 11" x 17". Acrylic Paints. Collection of El Rancho de las Golondrinas, La Cienega, New Mexico. In Museum's Morada. Photo by Anthony Richardson.

RIGHT: Jesús Nazareno bulto with andas or litter for carrying in procession, 1990. Size: 22" tall. Cottonwood, mineral pigments. Part of the traveling exhibition Images of Penance, Images of Mercy. Collection of and photo by the Taylor Museum for Southwestern Studies of the Colorado Springs Fine Arts Center.

TOP: La Santísima Trinidad/The Holy Trinity retablo, 1989. Size: 11" x 14.5". Note similarities to piece by José Rafael Aragón in William Wroth's <u>Christian Images in Hispanic New Mexico</u>, page 151, plate 127. Collection of Barbara and Bill Douglas. Photo by Robert Reck.

BOTTOM: Cristo head bulto, 1990. Size: 6" tall. Collection of George and Julianna Alderman. Photo by Ron Behrmann.

LEFT: Jesús Nazareno bulto with andas or litter for carrying in procession, 1989. Size: 23" tall. Collection of George and Julianna Alderman. Photo by Ron Behrmann.

> "In these times of consumer capitalism, where whoever dies with the most things wins, Charlie has a different reason to be alive."
>
> Thomas Steele, S.J.

TOP: Santiago retablo, 1986. Size: 11.75" x 13.5". Collection of Millicent Rogers Museum, Taos, New Mexico. Photo by artist.

RIGHT: San Acacio bulto, retablo and cross, 1987. Size: 16" tall. The feet are tied together with yucca fiber/cord. Regis University Collection of New Mexican Santos, Denver. Photo by Thomas Steele, S.J.

Father Thomas Steele commissioned Charlie to do this piece for the Regis University Collection of New Mexican Santos. This was Charlie's first retablo/bulto combination piece. The inspiration for this piece was José Rafael Aragón; see E. Boyd's Popular Arts of Spanish New Mexico, page 359, plate 24 and William Wroth's Christian Images in Hispanic New Mexico, plate 141.

TOP: Escudo de San Francisco/Shield of Saint Francis retablo, 1994. Size: 5.5" x 9.5". Private Collection. Photo by Ron Behrmann.

LEFT: Relicario/Monstrance, 1992. Two retablos on sides – Virgin Mary and Saint Joseph kneeling. Size: 23.5" tall. Center reliquary holds figure of Christ. Charlie sees this piece more as a Nacimiento or Nativity piece with the Holy Family – Christ the central symbol at Christmas as well as throughout the year. Exhibited as a part of the Albuquerque Museum <u>Charles M. Carrillo: Santos</u> show in 1993 to celebrate "The Year of American Craft: A Celebration of the Creative Work of the Hand." This piece was modeled after a monstrance by José Rafael Aragón in the San Antonio Chapel in Córdova, New Mexico. See Larry Frank's <u>New Kingdom of the Saints</u>, page 235, plate 221. Private Collection. Photo by Robert Reck.

TOP: Nuestra Señora de los Dolores retablo, 1991. Size: 5.75" x 9.5". Private Collection. Photo by Craig Varjabedian.

RIGHT: Cristo Crucificado/Nuestra Señora de los Dolores double-sided retablo, 1991. Size: 16" x 12.75". Robin Farwell Gavins' *Traditional Arts of Spanish New Mexico*, page 81. Exhibited in the Heard Museum's *¡Chispas!* traveling show. Private Collection. Photo by Craig Varjabedian.

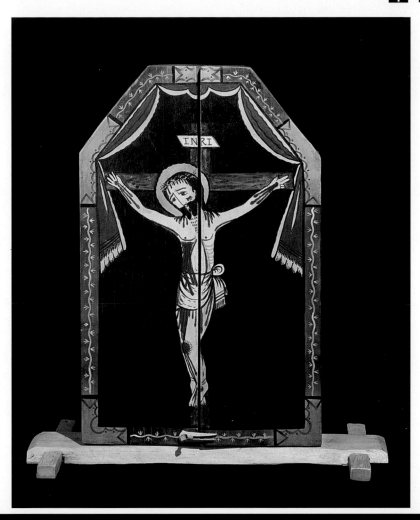

TOP: La Sagrada Corazon/The Sacred Heart retablo, 1986. Size: 5.75" x 5.5". Private Collection. Photo by Craig Varjabedian.

LEFT: Cristo Crucificado/Santa María Magdalena triptych retablo, 1993. Size: 14" x 23"; with doors open 28" x 23"; base 21" wide by 10.5" deep. As piece is opened, Mary Magdalene appears coming out of Christ's heart with God the Father positioned above her. When fully opened, there are three tableaus of Mary Magdalene the Penitent caring for Christ. Private Collection. Photo by Robert Reck.

ABOVE: Cristo Crucificado retablo, 1990. Size: 15.25" x 20". Designed after Fresquís, the Truchas Master. Pine and mineral pigments. Part of traveling exhibition <u>Images of Penance, Images of Mercy</u>. Collection of and photo by the Taylor Museum for Southwestern Studies of the Colorado Springs Fine Arts Center.

TOP: Cristo Crucificado retablo, 1989. Size: 8.5" x 15.5". Based on design by Pedro Antonio Fresquís, 1749-1831. Private Collection. Photo by owner.

BOTTOM: Cristo Crucificado retablo, 1990. Size: 5" x 9". Collection of Barbara and Bill Douglas. Photo by Robert Reck.

ABOVE: Cristo Crucificado retablo, 1989. Size: 11" x 15". Based on design by Fresquís. Collection of Jennifer Martinez and William McArthur. Photo by Robert Reck.

TOP: Cristo Crucificado retablo, 1991. Size: 14" x 20". Collection of Sandra Banstorp. Photo by Ebbe Banstorp.

BOTTOM: Cristo Crucificado retablo, 1992. Size: 4" x 8.5". Collection of Jennifer Martinez and William McArthur. Photo by Robert Reck.

TOP LEFT: Painted Cross, 1989. Size: 6" x 10". Collection of Sandra Banstorp. Photo by Ebbe Banstorp.

TOP RIGHT: Painted Cross, 1988. Size: 18.5" x 30". This is the first in a series of painted crosses depicting a narrative. It was inspired by a Pedro Antonio Fresquís piece in the Smithsonian collection, see Marta Weigle's Hispanic Arts & Ethnohistory, *page 248, figure 6; it was destroyed in a fire in the 60's. It depicts the birth of Christ, God the Father holding His Son in the crucifixion with Mary below. There is dripping blood down the sides of the cross. The wavy lines are uncharacteristic of Charlie's work. Collection of Paul and Nancy Pletka. Photo by Ron Behrmann.*

BOTTOM RIGHT: Painted Cross, 1986. Size: 36" x 48". Black background with large central panel depicting God the Father holding crucified Christ in his arms and Nuestra Señora de los Dolores beneath God's feet. Bottom of cross has two blue robed angels holding host pierced by red and black nails. Three tin conchas at ends on arms and at bottom. Straw applique around the halo. Based on design by Fresquís. International Folk Art Foundation Collection at the Museum of International Folk Art, Santa Fe, NM. Photo by Blair Clark.

TOP: Cristo Crucificado bulto, 1991. Size: 13" x 23" cross; 11" Cristo. Private Collection. Photo by Craig Varjabedian.

BOTTOM: Cristo head retablo, 1989. Size: 11" x 16". Private Collection. Photo by Craig Varjabedian.

LEFT: Cristo Crucificado bulto, 1992. Size: 18" tall. Presented to the Abiquiú Morada on its re-dedication in 1993. Photo by Craig Varjabedian.

TOP: *Cristo Crucificado retablo,
1990. Size: 5.75" x 11". See Christine
Mather's* Colonial Frontiers, *page 23,
figure 39 for the inspiration for this
piece. Private Collection. Photo by
Craig Varjabedian.*

RIGHT: *Calvario: Cristo Crucificado
con San Juan Evangelista y La Virgin
bulto, 1989. Size: 19.5" x 27.25".
Charlie was inspired by a piece by
José Aragón for this bulto. See
William Wroth's* Christian Images
in Hispanic New Mexico, *page 127,
plate 95. Collection of Paul and
Nancy Pletka. Photo by Kirk
Gittings.*

*This was the last crucifix that Charlie carved while still living in Albuquerque. This is the
only one done with two mourning figures in three-dimensional form at the base of the
cross. It is influenced by José Rafael Aragón. A "Calvario" is the name for a scene from
Calvary. Sometimes Mary Magdelene may be also present but in New Mexico that is
very rare. The historical background goes back to medieval paintings that were used for
teaching purposes.*

TOP: Cristo Crucificado retablo, 1990. Size: 5.5" x 9". Design on border derived from *Jemez Pueblo Marriage Book*, 1720. Collection of Jennifer Martinez and William McArthur. Photo by Robert Reck.

LEFT: Cristo Crucificado bulto in nicho, 1989. Size: 12" tall Cristo and cross; nicho 16" tall. The nicho and crucifix were done separately and both were put together by the owner. The blue Cristo is one of the smallest Charlie has done and the influence goes back to medieval times. When a body was hung on a cross it would turn blue from shock — cyanotic. The Penitentes thought a body would turn blue from the cold of Easter in Northern New Mexico. Collection of Paul and Nancy Pletka. Photo by Ron Behrmann.

TOP LEFT: Cristo Crucificado retablo, 1991. Size: 8.5" x 10". Private Collection. Photo by Craig Varjabedian.

MIDDLE: Cristo Crucificado bulto, 1990. Size: 20" tall. Collection of Barbara and Bill Douglas. Photo by Robert Reck.

BOTTOM RIGHT: Cristo Crucificado bulto, 1990. Size: 12.5" tall. Blue tone and eyes closed as a medieval symbol for death. Collection of Barbara and Bill Douglas. Photo by Robert Reck.

TOP LEFT: Painted cross, 1993. Cristo Crucificado y Nuestra Señora de los Dolores with prayer inset: "Oh Dios mío que en el admirable Sacramento nos dejasteis la memoria de vuestra Pasíon, concedednos como os pedimos, que de tal manera veneremos los misterios de vuestro Cuerpo y Sangre que perennemente sintamos en nosotros el fruto de vuestra redención, Vos que vivís y reináis por los siglos y siglos. Amén." Size: 18" x 34.5". Private Collection. Photo by Ron Behrmann.

MIDDLE: Corazon de Nuevo Mexico painted cross, 1993. Size: 16" x 24". Charlie's wife Debbie suggested the vines on the cross. They represent the tree of life. Authors' Collection. Photo by Ron Behrmann.

TOP RIGHT: Cristo Crucificado retablo, 1991. Size: 5.75" x 9". See Thomas Steele's _Santos and Saints_, page 38 for a similar retablo by Pedro Antonio Fresquís. Private Collection. Photo by Craig Varjabedian.

TOP: *Nuestra Señora de la Imaculada Concepción retablo, 1994. Size: 13.75" x 25". Collection of Barbara and Bill Douglas. Photo by Ron Behrmann.*

BOTTOM: *San José retablo, 1991. Size: 6" x 10". Collection of Ron and Trish Behrmann. Photo by Ron Behrmann.*

RIGHT: *Reredos/Altar screen of San José con Niño, 1990. Size: 19" x 48". Private Collection. Photo by Craig Varjabedian.*

ABOVE: Reredos/Altar screen, 1990. Size: 53" x 61". The iconography for this reredos was designed by the owner. From the top the images are: La Santisima Trinidad; (1st row) San Miguel, the Creation of Eve from Adam's rib, the Ressurection of Christ, Noah's Ark, and Moses with the tablets of God surrounded by the flames; (second row) the Annunciation, the Nacimiento or Manger, Christ in the garden, the Temptation of Christ, and Christ speaking to Mary Magdalene; (bottom row) the Transfiguration, the Flagellation of Christ, the Descent into Hades, and Christ's Descent from the Cross. Charlie calls this piece "Unfinished Business." Private Collection. Photo by Robert Reck.

TOP: San Isidro retablo, 1986. Size: 11" x 17". Retablo also contains (clockwise from upper left) San José, Nuestra Señora de Guadalupe, San Felipe de Jesús and San Miguel; these images depict the agricultural seasons and the patron saint of the recipient. Collection of Felipe Mirabal. Photo by Ron Behrmann.

TOP: Nuestra Señora de Guadalupe retablo, 1991. Size: 8.75" x 14". Collection of Professor and Mrs. Samuel Roberson. Photo by Craig Varjabedian.

BOTTOM: San José retablo, 1993. Size: 11.75" x 12". Collection of Professor and Mrs. Samuel Roberson. Photo by owner.

ABOVE: Reredos/Altar screen with San Isidro, 1992. Inset images are of San Rafael and Nuestra Señora del Loretto. Size: 35.5" x 48". Gift to artist's parents when they moved back to father's ancestral farm in Abeytas, New Mexico. Exhibited as a part of the Albuquerque Museum <u>Charles M. Carrillo: Santos</u> show in 1993 to celebrate "The Year of American Craft: A Celebration of the Creative Work of the Hand." Photo by Robert Reck.

ABOVE: Reredos/Altar screen, 1994. Size: 114" x 120". The reredos/altar screen in the Golondrinas Placita Chapel is dedicated to San Isidro Labrador, because of his patronage of the agricultural and pastoral lifestyles of thLos Golondrinas living museum. Altar screens often depicted the life of Christ, the life of the Virgin Mary or the life and/or martyrdom of a particular saint. This reredos contains the following clockwise from top center: La Santísima Trinidad, La Sagrada Familia, San Miguel Arcangel, San Isidro Labrador y Santa María Toribia de la Cabeza, San Antonio Abad, San Luís Gonzaga, San Isidro Labrador bulto, Señor San José Patriarca, San Pascual Bailón, Santa Inés del Campo, and Nuestra Señora de Guadalupe. The altar table, painted by Charlie Carrillo features the Eucharistic symbols of grapes and wheat on the right and Agnus Dei/The Lamb of God on the left. Charlie also painted the crown or lunette. The reredos in the chapel in the Golondrinas Placita was a collaborative project with iconography designed by Felipe Mirabal, curator of museum collections, and eleven santeros: Luís Tapia, Alcario Otero, Victor Goler, Eduardo Sanchez, Ernie Lujan, David Nabor Lucero, Jacobo de la Serna, Ramón José López, Irene Martinez-Yates, James Cordova, and Charlie Carrillo. Collection of El Rancho de las Golondrinas housed in the Golondrinas Placita Chapel. The altar was funded by the Oliver S. and Jennie R. Donaldson Charitable Trust of New York. Photo by Jack Parsons.

TOP: Reredos/Altar screen, 1982. Size: 25" x 48". Clockwise from upper right: the images include San Miguel, San José, Santa Barbara, San Francisco, Nuestra Señora de Carmen, and San Rafael. The center top is La Santisima Trinidad/The Holy Trinity and Santo Niño de Atocha in the center. Acrylic paints. Collection of El Rancho de las Golondrinas. Photo by Anthony Richardson.

TOP: Nuestra Señora de Guadalupe retablo, 1987. Size: 20.5" x 32". Collection of David and Deborah Berardinelli. Photo by Ron Behrmann.

BOTTOM: San José Patriarca retablo, 1987. Size: 20.5" x 30.5". Collection of David and Deborah Berardinelli. Photo by Ron Behrmann.

RIGHT: Reredos/Altar screen, 1991. Size: 9.5" x 10.5". Clockwise from upper left: the images include San Francisco, Santa María Magdalena, San Geronimo, and Santa Rosa. Collection of Jennifer Martinez and William McArthur. Photo by Robert Reck.

TOP: Nuestra Señora de los Afligidos retablo, 1989. Size: 4.5" x 7.5". See Christine Mather's <u>Colonial Frontiers</u>, page 22, figure 36. Private Collection. Photo by Ron Behrmann.

BOTTOM: Cristo retablo, 1991. Size: 5.5" x 9". Private Collection. Photo by Craig Varjabedian.

LEFT: Cristo on hide, 1990. Size: 16" x 18". Collection of Jennifer Martinez and William McArthur. Photo by Robert Reck.

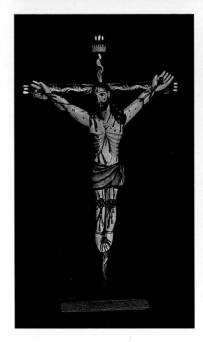

TOP: Detail of Cristo Crucificado bulto, 1991. Size: 14" tall. Usually displayed in the Altar de Penitencia at right. Photo by Ron Behrmann.

RIGHT: Reredos/Altar de Penitencia with Cristo Crucificado bulto, 1991. Size: 40.5" x 88". Clockwise from top center: the images include La Santísima Trinidad, Nuestra Señora de los Dolores, Arma Cristi, Cristo Crucificado, El Sagrador Corazón y las Cinco Llagas, and San Francisco. A carved dove is hanging just below La Santísima Trinidad. Exhibited as a part of the Heard Museum ¡Chispas! show in 1991, the Albuquerque Museum Charles M. Carrillo: Santos show in 1993 and the Harwood Foundation Seis Santeros show in 1994. Private Collection. Photo by Ron Behrmann.

THE RESOURCES

Permanent Collections

Albuquerque International Airport, Albuquerque, New Mexico – public art collection, lower terminal (Ross Airlines) Flight From Egypt retablo (1988).

Albuquerque Museum, Albuquerque, New Mexico – San Felipe de Jesús bulto (1993) and San Isidro de Labradór retablo (1993).

Archdiocese of Santa Fe Catholic Center Chapel, Albuquerque, New Mexico – Stations of the Cross (1987).

Denver Art Museum, Denver, Colorado – San Isidro retablo (1993).

Gene Autry Western Heritage Museum, Los Angeles, California – San Isidro Labrador. Grand Prize, 1990 Spanish Market (1990).

The Heard Museum, Phoenix, Arizona – Nuestra Señora de los Siete Dolores hollow-frame bulto. Exhibited in ¡Chispas! show. (1991).

King Juan Carlos and the People of Spain – Retablo (1987) "Fe de Nuestros Antepasados/Faith of Our Ancestors" presented in Santa Fe. Suite of the Tamarind Lithographs presented by the Greater New Mexico Quintocentenario Committee in 1991.

Our Lady of Perpetual Help Church, Albuquerque, New Mexico – Eleven Byzantine retablos (1986), Raising of Lazarus, The Holy Prophet Elias, Saint Stephen, Holy Trinity, Saints Peter & Paul, Saint Mary Magdalene & the Risen Savior, All Souls, Saint Michael, Saint John the Baptist, Our Lady of the Sign, The Protection of the Mother of God.

The Lady of Guadalupe Chapel, The Diocese of Las Cruces Pastoral Center, Las Cruces, New Mexico – Six retablos commissioned for the Diocese's 10th anniversary – San Francisco, San Isidro, Santo Niño de Atocha, Santa Rita, San José, and San Lorenzo (1992).

St. Meinrad Archabbey, St. Meinrad, Indiana – Nuestra Señora de Guadalupe retablo.

Mexican Fine Arts Center Museum, Chicago, Illinois – Nuestra Señora de Guadalupe retablo.

Millicent Rogers Museum, Taos, New Mexico – Set of Tamarind Institute prints, San Isidro Labrador retablo (1986) with straw applique by Jimmy Trujillo. Santiago retablo (1986). Not on permanent exhibit.

Mt. Angel Abbey and Seminary, St Benedict, Oregon – Nuestra Señora de Guadalupe retablo (1989).

Museum of International Folk Art, Santa Fe, New Mexico – "Holy Family" after a 19th Century retablo by José Rafael Aragón, exhibited on the wall at the entrance of the Hispanic Heritage Wing, a set of Tamarind Institute Santeros Prints (2) and several crosses and retablos. One of Debbie's pots is also in the Spanish Colonial Arts Society collection housed at the Museum.

The National Museum of American History, Smithsonian Institution, Washington, D.C. – elk hide painting done for American Encounters exhibit of Saint Joseph and the Christ Child, (1990).

Palace of the Governors, Santa Fe, New Mexico – Six Hide Paintings in the Prince Room.

El Rancho de las Golondrinas, La Cienega, Santa Fe, New Mexico – A living history museum of Hispanic culture. There are three pieces of Charlie's, one in the Morada and one in the Oratorio or family chapel. Both pieces are very early. Charlie was also one of the participants in a new altar screen/reredos that was finished in June 1994 and funded by the Oliver S. & Jennie R. Donaldson Charitable Trust.

Ojo Caliente Church, Ojo Caliente, New Mexico – Reredos with six santeros (1994)

Regis University, Denver, Colorado – San Acacio bulto con retablo (1987), San José retablo (1987) and work by Charlie's children. Exhibit located in the library.

TOP: First Station of the Cross, 1994. Size: 14" x 21.5" Santa María de la Paz Catholic Community, Santa Fe. Photo by Craig Varjabedian.

BOTTOM: Second Station of the Cross, 1994. Size: 14" x 21.5" Santa María de la Paz Catholic Community, Santa Fe. Photo by Craig Varjabedian.

TOP: *Third Station of the Cross, 1994. Size: 14" x 21.5" Santa María de la Paz Catholic Community, Santa Fe. Photo by Craig Varjabedian.*

BOTTOM: *Fourth Station of the Cross, 1994. Size: 14" x 21.5" Santa María de la Paz Catholic Community, Santa Fe. Photo by Craig Varjabedian.*

President Salinas de Gortari and the People of Mexico – Suite of the Tamarind Lithographs presented by the Greater New Mexico Quintocentenario Committee in 1991.

Sacred Heart Church, Colorado Springs, Colorado – altar screen (1993).

Santa María de la Paz Catholic Community, Santa Fe – Saint Joseph bulto (gift from the Carrillo family to their parish church) and 14 Stations of the Cross (1994).

Spanish Colonial Arts Society, Santa Fe, New Mexico – San Isidro Labrador retablo (1991). Stored at the Museum of International Folk Art, Santa Fe, New Mexico.

The Taylor Museum for Southwestern Studies of the Colorado Springs Fine Arts Center, Colorado Springs, Colorado – Jesús Nazareno bulto, (1990) & Cristo Crucificado (after the Truchas Master) retablo (1990). Both are featured in the traveling exhibit Images of Penance, Images of Mercy.

White House President's Gift Collection, Washington, DC – San Ignacio de Loyola retablo (1988). Presented to President Bill Clinton by Regis University during his visit with Pope John Paul II in August 1993.

Woodbourne Correctional Facility, Woodbourne, New York – Nuestra Señora de Guadalupe retablo (1991).

Bibliography Part I: Santos and Santeros

Albuquerque Monthly, January/February 1989, Hispanic Arts.

Ahlborn, Richard Eighme, The Penitente Moradas of Abiquiú, 1986, Smithsonian Institution Press, Washington and London.

Boyd, E., Saints and Saintmakers of New Mexico, 1946, Laboratory of Anthropology, Santa Fe.

Boyd, E., Popular Arts of Spanish New Mexico, 1974, Museum of New Mexico Press, Santa Fe.

Boyd, E., "The Literature of Santos", 1950, reprinted from the Spring issue of Southwest Review, Southern Methodist University Press, Dallas.

Briggs, Charles L., The Wood Carvers of Córdova, 1980, University of Tennessee Press, Knoxville.

Chavez, Fray Angelico, La Conquistadora, 1975, 1983, Sunstone Press, Santa Fe.

Dickey, Roland F., New Mexico Village Arts, 1949, 1970, University of New Mexico Press, Albuquerque.

El Palacio, Magazine of the Museum of NM, Winter 1992/93. Article on the "Across Generations" exhibit featuring work by Roán & Estrellita Carrillo.

Espinosa, José E., Saints in the Valleys, 1960, The University of New Mexico Press, Albuquerque.

Frank, Larry, New Kingdom of the Saints, 1992, Red Crane Books, Santa Fe.

Gavin, Robin Farwell, Traditional Arts of Spanish New Mexico: The Hispanic Hertigae Wing at the Museum of International Folk Art, 1994, Museum of New Mexico Press, Santa Fe.

Hamilton, Nancy, Retablo Newsletter, El Paso, Texas.

Kalb, Laurie Beth, Santos, Statues & Sculpture: Contemporary Woodcarving from New Mexico, 1988, Craft and Folk Art Museum, Los Angeles.

Martinez, Eluid Levi, What is a New Mexican Santo? 1978, reprinted 1992, Sunstone Press, Santa Fe.

Mather, Christine, Colonial Frontiers: Art & Life in Spanish New Mexico The Fred Harvey Collection, 1983, Ancient City Press, Santa Fe.

Mexico: Splendor of Thirty Centuries, 1990, Metropolitan Museum of Art, Bullfinch Press, New York.

Mills, George, The People of the Saints, 1967, The Taylor Museum of the Colorado Springs Fine Arts Center, Colorado Springs.

Pino, Pedro Bautista, From The New World, Life & Times, To Be Published 1994, UNM Press and El Rancho de las Golondrinas – originally published in 1812 with 1930 translation.

Sacred Land: Indian and Hispanic Cultures of the Southwest. Taylor Museum for Southwestern Studies of the Colorado Springs Fine Arts Center, Colorado Springs.

Santos of the Southwest: The Denver Art Museum Collection, 1970, A. B. Hirschfeld Press.

The Santero's Art of Historic New Mexico: 1760-1960, The Priscilla Timpson Collection, exhibited at Al Luckett Jr. & Morning Star Gallery in Santa Fe. Essay included by Marie Romero Cash, "The Santero's Art of Historic New Mexico 1760-1960."

Shalkop, Robert L., Wooden Saints, The Santos of New Mexico, 1967, The Taylor Museum of the Colorado Springs Fine Arts Center, Colorado Springs.

Spanish Market Magazine, An annual publication of The Spanish Colonial Arts Society.

Steele, S.J., Thomas J., <u>Santos and Saints: The Religious Folk Art of Hispanic New Mexico</u>, 1974, 1982, revised 1994, Ancient City Press, Santa Fe.

Wakely, David, and Thomas Drain, <u>A Sense of Mission</u>, 1994, Chronicle Books, San Francisco.

Weigle, Marta, Claudia Larcombe, and Samuel Larcombe, <u>Hispanic Arts and Ethnohistory</u>, 1983, The Spanish Colonial Arts Society, Ancient City Press, Santa Fe.

Wilder, Mitchell A., and Edgar Breitenbach, <u>Santos, The Religious Folk Art of New Mexico</u>, 1943, The Taylor Museum of the Colorado Springs Fine Arts Center, Colorado Springs.

Wroth, William, <u>Christian Images in Hispanic New Mexico</u>, 1982, The Taylor Museum of the Colorado Springs Fine Arts Center, Colorado Springs.

Wroth, William, <u>Hispanic Crafts of the Southwest</u>, 1977, The Taylor Museum of the Colorado Springs Fine Arts Center, Colorado Springs.

Wroth, William, <u>Images of Penance, Images of Mercy: Southwestern Santos in the Late Nineteenth Century</u>, 1991, University of Oklahoma Press, Norman.

Bibliography Part II: Publications by or Containing References to Charlie Carrillo

Baca, Elmo, and Suzanne Deats, <u>Santa Fe Design</u>, 1990, Beekman House, New York.

Beebe, Katharine, "La Muerte: She Lives!", <u>Mirage</u>, Winter 1994, University of New Mexico Alumni Association, Albuquerque.

Boss, Gayle, and Cheryl Hellner, <u>Santo Making in New Mexico</u> and the companion guide <u>Way of Sorrow, Way of Light</u>, 1991, Potter's House Press, Washington, D.C.

Carrillo, Charles M., "Abiquiú Reservoir Project," <u>The Ethno-history of the Abiquiú Reservoir Region</u>, 1985, U.S. Army Corps of Engineers, Albuquerque.

Carrillo, Charles M., "The Acequias of El Llano, NM" <u>Report to the Office of the Governor</u>, 1985, New Mexico Bureau of Mines and Mineral Resources, Socorro.

Carrillo, Charles M., "Archaelogical Survey of 12.5 miles of the Pecos River Road," <u>Final Report: The Historic Artifacts of QRA-NM SM 84</u> (4, 5, 6, 7), Quivira Research Center, University of New Mexico, Albuquerque.

Carrillo, Charles M., "Colored Earth: the Tradition," <u>Traditional Southwest: The Adobe and Folk Art Magazine</u>, Fall 1989.

Carrillo, Charles M., "A Grassroots Adventure in Archaeology," <u>La Comunidad: Design, Development, and Self Determination in Hispanic Communities</u>, 1982, National Endowment for the Arts, Design Arts Program, Partners for Livable Places, Washington, D.C.

Carrillo, Charles M., "Hispanic and Native American Ceramic Assemblages from LA 288," <u>Archaeological Testing and Analysis Along a Mountain Bell Cable Near Two Sites in Corrales, NM</u>, 1985, UNM Office of Contract Archaeology, Albuquerque.

Carrillo, Charles M., "Hispanic Sources" in <u>Sources and Inspirations: Paintings by Paul Pletka</u> 1990, Exhibition Catalogue, Museum of Fine Arts, Santa Fe.

Carrillo, Charles M., "My Tio Floyd," <u>Ghost Ranch Journal</u>, 1991, an article on Debbie Carrillo's uncle Floyd and his knowledge of Hispanic verbal history.

Carrillo, Charles M., <u>New Mexican Hispanic Pottery as Evidence of Craft Specialization, 1790-1890</u>; Dissertation in progress, University of New Mexico, Albuquerque.

Carrillo, Charles M., "Pottery of the Abiquiú Reservoir Area," <u>Archaeological and Historical Research at Abiquiú Reservoir</u>, 1987, U.S. Army Corps of Engineers, Albuquerque.

Carrillo, Charles M., <u>Ramilletes Del Papel</u> (Cut Paper Floral Bouquets), Manuscript written for the Spanish Colonial Arts Society.

Carrillo, Charles M., "Santos: A Brief History", <u>Santero Exhibition: The 1988 Taos Spring Arts Celebration</u>. 1988.

Carrillo, Charles M., "Traditional New Mexican Hispanic Crafts: Ayer Y Hoy — Yesterday and Today", <u>1991-92 The Wingspread Collector's Guide</u>.

Carrillo, Charles M., "Where Were the Sheep: The Piedra Lumbre Phases Revisited," 1993, New Mexico Archeological Society, Brad Viera, editor.

Carrillo, Charles M., and Christine A. Rudecoff, "Test Excavations at San Antonio de los Poblanos: A Spanish Colonial Community on the Middle Rio Grande," 1987, Archeological Society of New Mexico, Ancient City Press, Santa Fe.

<u>Dia de Los Muertos/Day of the Dead</u>, 1991, Mexican Fine Arts Center Museum, Chicago.

TOP: Fifth Station of the Cross, 1994. Size: 14" x 21.5" Santa María de la Paz Catholic Community, Santa Fe. Photo by Craig Varjabedian.

BOTTOM: Sixth Station of the Cross, 1994. Size: 14" x 21.5" Santa María de la Paz Catholic Community, Santa Fe. Photo by Craig Varjabedian.

Familia y Fe, 1989, KNME-TV, Albuquerque, *Colores!*

Flow of the River/Corre el Rio, Hispanic Culture Foundation, 1988 (San Rafael retablo, 1987).

El Palacio, The Magazine of the Museum of New Mexico, Winter 1977, "Abiquiú's Roots: Villagers Unearth Their Past."

El Palacio, The Magazine of the Museum of New Mexico, Summer, 1988.

En Divina Luz, 1990 KNME-TV, Albuquerque, by Karl Kernberger, Producer, *Colores!*

Guestlife New Mexico: 1994-95, 1994, "The Art of the Santeros."

Handcrafts, Fall 1993, *Carving Traditions.*

Hayden, Niki, Art in the West: A Legacy of Common People, 1993, Boulder Arts Commission.

Hispanic Heritage Wing, Museum of International Folk Art, CD1 Track 22, Las Inditas De Santo Tomás/Inditas Music of the Santo Tomas Fiesta (with Dexter & Floyd Trujillo). Charlie also appears on one of the video tapes in the *Familia y Fe* exhibit.

Kalb, Laurie Beth, Crafting Devotion: Tradition in Contemporary New Mexico Santos (to be published in December, 1994 by UNM Press) Can be obtained from the Gene Autry Western Heritage Museum, Los Angeles. Catalog of the exhibit.

La Iglesia de Santa Cruz, 1993, Published by ACCU Blueprint & Copy Center, Espanola, NM.

Morrison, Howard, American Encounters, 1992, The Smithsonian Institution.

Pardue, Diana, ¡Chispas!, Cultural Warriors of New Mexico, 1992, Phoenix, The Heard Museum.

Poling, Lesley, Coronas de Talco y Flores, Youth Magazine, January 1979.

Que Suave, KSBW Radio, Santa Fe, New Mexico. Guest: Charlie Carrillo, October 16, 1993.

Santero, KNME TV, 1991, Albuquerque, by Cindy Barchus, Producer, *Colores!*

Santeros Unidos (working title) Dave Ashmore, producer, independent film on santeros and Hispanic Crafts

Southwest Sampler, Christmas, 1991, *Carving Traditions.*

SPUR, The Newsletter for the Gene Autry Western Heritage Museum, January, 1991.

Steven, Clifford, and William Hart McNichols, Aloysius, 1993, Our Sunday Visitor Publishing Division, Huntington, IN.

Traditions Southwest, Fall 1989, The Adobe & Folk Art Magazine, "Colored Earth: The Tradition."

Varjabedian, Craig, and Michael Wallis, En Divina Luz: The Penitente Moradas of New Mexico, 1994. Afterword by Charlie Carrillo, University of New Mexico Press, Albuquerque.

Wozniak, Frank, Meade Kemrer, and Charles Carrillo, History and Ethnohistory Along the Rio Chama, 1992, U.S. Army Corps of Engineers, Albuquerque.

Lectures by Charlie Carrillo

1982 – New Mexico Folklore Society (Abiquiú), *Curios: Hispanic Practices Against Witchcraft;* New Mexico Artists in Residence Program (1982-90); Fall – Rancho de las Golondrinas (La Cienega, NM) Hispanic Heritage week, *Santos de Nuevo Mexico.*

1983 – Senior Arts Albuquerque; March – Piro Conference, Socorro, NM, *The Founding of Abeytas, NM, During the Late Spanish Colonial Period;* New Mexico State Fair, *Crafts of Yesteryear Series* (1983-88); August – Albuquerque Museum, Feria Artesana Lecture Series, *The Making of New Mexican Santos;* Winter – Ghost Ranch (Abiquiú), *Ethnohistory & Anthropology: A View Toward Cultural Awareness*

1984 – August – Albuquerque Museum, Feria Artesana Lecture Series, *The Making of New Mexican Santos;* October – Albuquerque Historical Society, *The Genizaro of New Mexico;* Rancho de las Golondrinas (La Cienega, NM) Hispanic Heritage week, *Santos de Nuevo Mexico*

1985 – May – The Rio Grande Institute, Scholarship Series Presentations (Taos), *Santo Niño de Atocha: A New Mexican Devotion;* June – UNM Lectures Under The Stars, *Hispanic Witchcraft in New Mexico: Folktales and Dog Tails;* Summer – Pecos National Monument Hispanic Craft Lecture Series, *New Mexico Santos: Cultural Continuum*

1986 – January – Austin College Ghost Ranch (Abiquiú) Seminars, *The Art & History of Hispanic New Mexico;* March – Santa Fe, *The Role of Penitentes in Their Communities . . . Ayer y Hoy*

1987 – The Mexican Center Fine Arts Museum (Chicago), *Santos and Santeros Tradition;* July – International Folk Art Museum, Hispanic Heritage Week; October – American Folklore Society Convention, *New Mexico Santero as an Educator*

TOP: *Seventh Station of the Cross, 1994. Size: 14" x 21.5" Santa María de la Paz Catholic Community, Santa Fe. Photo by Craig Varjabedian.*

BOTTOM: *Eighth Station of the Cross, 1994. Size: 14" x 21.5" Santa María de la Paz Catholic Community, Santa Fe. Photo by Craig Varjabedian.*

1988 – March – International Folk Art Museum, Demonstration of retablo carving for cast of Milagro Beanfield War; May – KNME-TV 5 (Albuquerque), Heirloom Discovery Day, *Spanish Folk Art*; June – Taos Spring Arts Celebration Santos Exhibit, Fechin Institute; June – American Craft Council Regional Assembly, *Ayer y Hoy*, University of Alabama, Tuscaloosa

1989 – October – The Mexican Center Fine Arts Museum (Chicago), *Dia de los Muertos in New Mexico*; Fall – New Mexico Highlands University, *Cross Cultural Dynamics of the Southwest* and *Historic Hispanic Archaeology of New Mexico*

1990 – February – Laboratory of Anthropology, *Hispanic Crafts of New Mexico*; April – Heard Museum Board of Directors, *Hispanic Crafts of New Mexico*; Summer – Crow Canyon Archeological Center, *Hispanic Arts Of Northern New Mexico*; October – Demonstration of santo carving at the Heard Museum, Phoenix; November – Indian Pueblo Cultural Center, Albuquerque, *Shared Traditions: Modern Expressions*

1991 – April – Old Taos Trade Fair, *The History of Santos and the Future of Hispanic Folk Art*; June – University of Northern Colorado summer series, *Voices of Dissent*; Summer – Demonstrations and lectures at El Rancho de las Golondrinas; July – The Hulbert Center for Southwestern Studies, The Colorado College; September – The Walters Arts Gallery, *The Living Tradition of Hispanic Southwestern Religious Art*; December – Ghost Ranch Conference Center, New Mexico Crafts & Cultures Maxiweek

1992 – February – The University of Oklahoma, Fred Jones, Jr. Art Center Museum of Art, *Images of Penance, Images of Mercy*, lecture and demonstration, also lecture demonstrations at the Taylor Museum, Colorado Springs and the Walters Art Gallery, Baltimore; Spring – University of New Mexico, Los Alamos, course, *Retablo Making*; May – NAEA Conference at the Heard, *Teaching Through Diversity: Leaps and Boundaries*; Pikes Peak Community College, *Images of Saints in Two Catholic Cultures*; June – McMichael Artists in Residence, D'Art Canadien, Ontario; Summer – Festival at the Mall, Washington D.C. (demonstrating and speaker)

1993 – May – Music of New Mexico in Santa Fe, San Isidro Historic Church, Corrales, NM; September – Professional Advancement Workshops for Traditional Spanish Market Artists by Charlie Carrillo & Ramón José López at Museum of International Folk Art; October – One Man Show, Albuquerque Museum; October – Pueblo (Colorado) Cultural Arts Center, Santo workshop; *A Celebration of Traditional Cultures*, New Mexico Folklife Festival, Las Cruces; November – The Denver Art Museum, *Materials & Techniques: Santos of Yesterday & Today*; December – The Kalamazoo Art League (Michigan), *New Mexican Saints, Today & Yesterday*; December – Palace of the Governors, Santa Fe, *Santos & Saints, A New Mexico Holiday Tradition*

1994 – February – Santa Fe Community College (Albuquerque) *Santos*; March – *Insights into the Creative Mind*, Arizona Commission on the Arts, Scottsdale; April – Folk Art Close Up, The Houston Seminar in Santa Fe; Santa Fe Community College: *Roadside Crosses in North Central New Mexico*; May – Maxwell Museum Association Annual Meeting, Keynote Speaker *The Santero Tradition and Continuity*; Harwood Foundation, Taos and Our Lady of Sorrows Catholic Church, Las Vegas (NM): *Roadside Crosses in North Central New Mexico*; June – Salina Arts and Humanities Commission, Salina, Kansas; August – *Faith, Santos and Santeros*, El Rancho de las Gonolondrinas, Santa Fe

Exhibits of Charlie Carrillo's Work

1981 – Santa Fe Festival of the Arts

1983 – El Rancho de las Golondrinas, La Cienega, NM, *The New Mexican Santero*

1986 – Gallery One, Albuquerque; November – Weyrich Gallery; Folk Art New Mexico

1987 – February – The Mexican Museum, San Francisco, *From The Inside Out: Mexican Folk Art In A Contemporary Context* (Also lectured); March – Mexican Center Fine Arts Museum *Images of Faith: Religious Art of Mexico*; September – First Unitarian Church, Albuquerque, *Spiritus Sanctus – Sacred Spirits of the Southwest*; South Broadway Cultural Center, Albuquerque, *Nuevo Mexico, Si!*

1988 – Crow Canyon Archeological Center, Cortez, Colorado, lecturer four times a year (1988 to present); Martinez House Fall Festival, an exhibitor (1988 to present); El Rancho de las Golondrinas, Spring and Harvest Festivals (1988 to present); June – Taos Spring Arts Celebration Santos Exhibit at Fechin Institute

1989 – Mexican Fine Arts Center Museum, Chicago, *El Dia de Los Muertos* (Debbie & Charlie invited to create a home altar; they made an Oreda dedicated to their relatives); July – The Opening of The Hispanic Heritage Wing, The Museum of International Folk Art, Santa

TOP: Ninth Station of the Cross, 1994. Size: 14" x 21.5" Santa María de la Paz Catholic Community, Santa Fe. Photo by Craig Varjabedian.

BOTTOM: Tenth Station of the Cross, 1994. Size: 14" x 21.5" Santa María de la Paz Catholic Community, Santa Fe. Photo by Craig Varjabedian.

TOP: Eleventh Station of the Cross, 1994. Size: 14" x 21.5" Santa María de la Paz Catholic Community, Santa Fe. Photo by Craig Varjabedian.

BOTTOM: Twelfth Station of the Cross, 1994. Size: 14" x 21.5" Santa María de la Paz Catholic Community, Santa Fe. Photo by Craig Varjabedian.

Fe, with exhibits *Familia Y Fe and Tradición De Orgullo* (1989 to present); Fall — New Mexico Highlands University Donnelly Library Gallery, one man show; November — *Charlie Carrillo, Ramón Móntee and Horacio Valdez*, Móntez Gallery I, Santa Fe

1990 — Summer — Center for the Arts of the Southwest, Santa Fe, *From Folk to Fine: Hispanic Artists of Northern New Mexico*

1991 — June — University of Northern Colorado Mariani Gallery, *Voices of Dissent;* Tamarind Institute, Albuquerque, *Tamarind Invites: Lithographs by New Mexican Santeros* exhibited at the Museum of International Folk Art; *¡Chispas! Cultural Warriors of New Mexico* Exhibition, Heard Museum, Phoenix, Arizona; Society for Contemporary Crafts, Pittsburgh, Pennsylvania, and Erie Art Museum, Erie, Pennsylvania; September — *New Mexican Woodcarvers*, University of California at San Diego; *Images of Penance, Images of Mercy: Southwestern Santos in the Late Nineteenth Century*, Walters Gallery, Baltimore, The University of Oklahoma, Fred Jones Jr. Art Center Museum of Art, Norman, Taylor Museum for Southwestern Studies, Colorado Springs, Danville, California, and Kleinburg, Ontario.

1992 — Fullerton, California Art Gallery; The Smithsonian Institution, *American Encounters* (Señor San José y El Santo Niño, 1990)

1993 — July — *Selections from the Spanish Colonial Arts Society and Traditional Spanish Market*, Governor's Gallery, State Capitol, Santa Fe; October — *Miniatures '93*, Albuquerque Museum; October — *Charles M. Carrillo: Santos*, one in a series of exhibitions held to celebrate "1993: The Year of American Craft, A Celebration of the Creative Work of the Hand," The Albuquerque Museum

1994 — January — Harwood Foundation, Taos, *Seis Santeros;* Jonson Gallery, University of New Mexico, *Visiting Artists;* June — Dedication of Stations and San José bulto at Santa María de la Paz Catholic Community, Santa Fe; The Smoky Hill River Festival, Salina, Kansas; Installation of altar piece at El Rancho de las Golondrinas (done with other santeros); *Santeros Unidos*, Móntez Gallery II, Santa Fe; October — Taylor Museum's *Images of Penance, Images of Mercy* scheduled in Pasadena (also scheduled to travel to Las Cruces and Albuquerque); December — *Cuando Hablan los Santos*, an exhibit of work of 12 santeros, guest curated by Charlie at the UNM Maxwell Museum of Anthropology (tentatively scheduled); *Crafting Devotion: Tradition in Contemporary New Mexican Santos* at the Gene Autry Western Heritage Museum, Los Angeles Dec. 1994 to Feb. 1995. Travels to other locations.

Honors & Awards

Charles Michael Carrillo
Participant in Spanish Market 1981 to present

1994 — E. Boyd Memorial Award for originality and expressive design: Nuestra Señora del Pueblito Querétero hollowframe bulto
    Florence Dibell Bartlett Award for innovative design, International Folk Art Foundation: San Isidro Labrador gesso relief retablo

1993 — First Place: Nuestra Señora de la Immaculada Concepción gesso relief retablo

1992 — First Place (First time Gesso relief exhibited): San Gerónimo gesso relief retablo

1991 — E. Boyd Memorial Award for originality and expressive design: Nuestra Señora de los Siete Dolores/Soledad bulto

1990 — Grand Prize Best of Show Award: San Isidro Labrador bulto

1989 — Hispanic Heritage Award for in-depth research, International Folk Art Foundation

1988 — Hispanic Heritage Award for in-depth research, International Folk Art Foundation

1987 — Hispanic Heritage Award for in-depth research, International Folk Art Foundation

1986 — Honorable Mention: San José retablo

1985 — Second Place Retablo

1984 — Merit Award for overall work

1981 — Second Place: La Muerte bulto

Other Festivals

1981 — 2nd Place for La Muerte (Death Cart), Santa Fe Festival of the Arts

Other Honors

1994 — Named one of Phoenix Home & Garden Magazine's "Masters of the Southwest"

1993 — Retablo presented to President Bill Clinton by Regis University, Denver, Colorado

1990 — Scholarship recipient, Tamarind Institute of Lithography, University of New Mexico
1987 — Spanish Market Poster, La Huida a Egipto. "Fe de Nuestros Antepasados" retablo presented
to King Juan Carlos and Queen Sophia of Spain at the Museum of International Folk Art
1983 — Scholarship recipient from the Rio Grande Institute for research on Santa Niño de Atocha
1981-83 — Scholarship recipient, Stephen Hammon Anthropological Scholarship, UNM
KiMo Theater Poster for La Compañia de Teatro De Albuquerque: "El Mas Pequeño de Mis Hijos"

Debbie Barbara Eliza Trujillo Carrillo
Participant in Spanish Market 1991 to present

Estrellita de Atocha Carrillo
Participant in Spanish Market 1985 to present
1989 — First Place/Under 12: Nuestra Señora de Guadalupe retablo
1988 — Honorable Mention/Under 12: Nuestra Señora de los Dolores retablo

Roán Miguel Carrillo
Participant in Spanish Market 1990 to present
1994 — Honorable Mention/Ages 9-13: Nuestra Señora de los Dolores bulto
1993 — First Place/Under 12: San Francisco de Asís bulto

Information on New Mexican Hispanic Culture

Albuquerque Museum
Albuquerque, New Mexico

Los Colores Museum
Corrales, New Mexico. Dedicated to the weaving traditions of New Mexico.

The Denver Art Museum
Denver, Colorado. Spanish Colonial Galleries.

Gene Autry Western Heritage Museum
Los Angeles, California. Crafting Devotion: Tradition in Contemporary New Mexican Santos will
open December 10, 1994. Charlie's Nuestra Señora del Pueblito Querétero hollowframe
bulto (winner of the E. Boyd Memorial Award for originality and expressive design at the
1994 Spanish Market) is tentatively scheduled to be part of the exhibit. The exhibit will be
available to travel to other museums after February 12, 1995.

Harwood Foundation
Taos, New Mexico. Collection of New Mexican santos.

Heard Museum
Phoenix, Arizona. ¡Chispas! exhibit has travelled around the country. In addition to works by Charlie
Carrillo, it exhibited materials from Eppie Archuleta, Teresa Archuleta-Sagel, Marie Romero
Cash, Juanita Jaramillo-Lavadie, Félix López, José Benjamín López, Ramón José López, Wilbert
Miera, Luís Tapia, Irvin Trujillo, María Vergara-Wilson, and Frederico Vigil.

Maxwell Museum of Anthropology
University of New Mexico, Albuquerque, New Mexico. Cuando Hablan los Santos exhibit, sched-
uled to open winter 1994, guest curated by Charlie Carrillo. In addition to works by Charlie
Carrillo, this exhibits material from Victor Goler, Luicito Lujan, Anita Romero Jones, Manuel
López, Leroy López, Félix López, Gloria López, José Benjamín López, Ramón José López,
Sabanita López Ortíz, and Marie Romero Cash. It will travel to other museums after its
initial exhibition.

Millicent Rogers Museum
Taos, New Mexico

Móntez Gallery
Santa Fe, New Mexico. A wide selection of contemporary Hispanic Art. The owner is well in-
formed and helpful.

Museo de las Americas
Denver, Colorado

TOP: Thirteenth Station of the Cross, 1994. Size: 14" x 21.5" Santa María de la Paz Catholic Community, Santa Fe. Photo by Craig Varjabedian.

BOTTOM: Fourteenth Station of the Cross, 1994. Size: 14" x 21.5" Santa María de la Paz Catholic Community, Santa Fe. Photo by Craig Varjabedian.

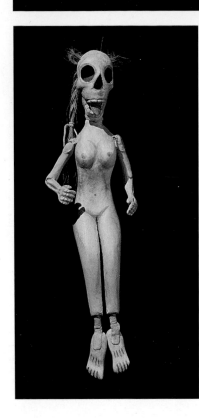

Museum of International Folk Art
Santa Fe, New Mexico. The largest collection of Spanish Colonial and Hispanic folk art in America. El Rio Abajo: Traditional Art from Southern New Mexico opens July 24, 1994.

The National Museum of American History, Smithsonian Institution
Washington, D.C. American Encounters exhibit 1992 through 2002.

Palace of the Governors Museum
Santa Fe, New Mexico. Permanent exhibits: Another Mexico: Spanish Life on the Upper Rio Grande and Society Defined: The Hispanic Resident of New Mexico, 1790.

El Rancho de las Golondrinas
La Cienega, New Mexico. Living History Museum, located south of Santa Fe, NM open from April through October. Special theme weekends include crafts and santos sold in a market atmosphere at festivals in June, August and October. Funded by the Oliver S. and Jennie R. Donaldson Charitable Trust of New York, a new altar screen for the Placita Chapel has been recently completed. It was a collaborative project with eleven *santeros* and designed by Charlie Carrillo: Luís Tapia, Alcario Otero, Victor Goler, Eduardo Sanchez, Ernie Lujan, David Nabor Lucero, Jacobo de la Serna, Ramón José López, Irene Martinez Yates, and James Cordova. The iconography of the altar screen was designed by Felipe Mirabal, the Curator of Collections at Las Golondrinas.

Regis University Collection of New Mexican Santos
Denver, Colorado. Collection of over 200 New Mexican santos from mid 1800s to present including: Molleno, José Aragón, José Rafael Aragón.

Santa Fe Council for the Arts
Santa Fe, New Mexico. Contemporary Spanish Market is held the same time as Traditional Spanish Market but booths are on several side streets near the Plaza. A different organization but the same goal — to promote the crafts of Hispanic New Mexico.

Southwest Museum
Los Angeles, California

Spanish History Museum
Albuquerque, New Mexico

Spanish Colonial Arts Society
Santa Fe, New Mexico. The Spanish Colonial Arts Society is a private, not-for-profit organization with membership open to the public. (505) 983-4038. Scheduled for release in December 1995, Spanish New Mexico: The Collections of the Spanish Colonial Arts Society. Spanish Market, held the last full weekend in July in the Plaza of Santa Fe. During Spanish Market, the Spanish Colonial Arts Society publishes a magazine that profiles exhibitors and lists all participants. Winter Spanish Market is held the first full weekend of December, traditionally in La Fonda Hotel, Santa Fe.

Taylor Museum of Southwestern Studies, Colorado Springs Fine Arts Center
Colorado Springs, Colorado. The exhibit, Images of Penance, Images of Mercy, curated by the Taylor Museum, has traveled to Walters Art Gallery (Baltimore), Fred Jones, Jr. Art Center Museum of Art (Norman), as well as Danville (California), Kleinburg (Ontario), Erie (Pennsylvania), and Pasadena (California). It is scheduled to travel to Las Cruces and Albuquerque (New Mexico) as well as Dallas (Texas).

TOP: Doña Sebestiana/Muerte bulto, 1993. Size: 18" tall. Private Collection. Photo by Robert Reck.

RIGHT: San Isidro Labrador with Santuario de Chimayo, retablo 1991. Size: 27" x 12". Exhibited as a part of Visiting Artists Show at Jonson Gallery, University of New Mexico in 1994. Authors' Collection. Photo by Ron Behrmann.